Grades 3–5

Math Bafflers

Logic Puzzles That Use Real-World Math

Grades 3–5

Math Bafflers

Logic Puzzles That Use Real-World Math

Marilynn L. Rapp Buxton

PRUFROCK PRESS INC.
WACO, TEXAS

Copyright © 2011, Prufrock Press Inc.

Edited by Sarah Morrison

Layout design by Raquel Trevino

Illustrations by Joshua Krezinski

ISBN-13: 978-1-59363-711-8

Printed in the United States of America.

At the time of this book's publication, all facts and figures cited are the most current available. All telephone numbers, addresses, and website URLs are accurate and active. All publications, organizations, websites, and other resources exist as described in the book, and all have been verified. The author and Prufrock Press Inc. make no warranty or guarantee concerning the information and materials given out by organizations or content found at websites, and we are not responsible for any changes that occur after this book's publication. If you find an error, please contact Prufrock Press Inc.

Prufrock Press Inc.
P.O. Box 8813
Waco, TX 76714-8813
Phone: (800) 998-2208
Fax: (800) 240-0333
http://www.prufrock.com

Table of Contents

Note to Teachers..1

How to Solve the Math Bafflers...3

Puzzles

Puzzles at the beginning of this list are easier to solve than the ones that come later in the list—but besides that, they are in no particular order. Puzzles at the end require you to use the logical thinking processes that you learned while solving the easier puzzles. Good luck!

The Dog Days of Summer (sequencing, time) 9

Halloween Haul (operations)...10

Show Me the Talent! (sequencing)..11

I Can "Ad" Fractions (fractions) 12

New Kids on the Block (age, time)..14

Breakfast Buddies (fractions)...15

Let's Party (inequalities)..16

Easter Eggscursion (inequalities) 17

What's for Lunch? (inequalities)..18

Natasha Knows Her Numbers (algebra)....................................20

It's a "Fun" Raiser (sequencing) 21

B. F. F. (numbers)...22

I'm on Cloud Nine (inequalities, multiples).............................23

Who Will Bee the Winner? (inequalities, logic).......................24

Test Out This Hat (inequalities, sequencing) 25

Tourney Trophy Time (ordering)...26

The Pumpkin Patches (weight measurement) 27

Let's Hang Out (operations)...28

Birthday in Buffalo (money)..29

Five Clubs (money) 30

Swing Sewing (distance measurement) 31

Time for Lunch (operations) 32

Waterford's Water Days (fractions)..33

Lucky Sevven (inequalities)...34

The Fine Art of Scheduling (time)...35

5K for Kendra (money, time) 36

Yummy, Yummy, Yummy, I Got Food in My Tummy (money)....37

Pick and Peck a Pie (fractions)..38

Table of Contents, continued

It's Quite the Quad-Athlon (time) 40

Let's Go to Quick Treats (money, weight measurement) 41

It's Not Pay Day, It's Field Day! (converting distances) 42

Holiday Vacation (sequencing) 44

Cross Country Craze (inequalities) 46

Greetings at the Meetings (sequencing) 47

Berry, Berry, Quite Culinary (fractions, volume measurement) 48

Kick, Pass, and Run (distance measurement) 50

Sisters Gone Shopping (money) 52

Fetch, Fido (distance measurement) 54

Solutions **56**

About the Author **83**

Note to Teachers

Many college professors and business professionals have told me, "Teach kids how to think and ask them to work hard." I teach elementary gifted and talented students in addition to teaching thinking skills in classrooms. Students in these classes learn creative thinking (e.g., fluency, flexibility, originality, elaboration, problem solving) and critical thinking (e.g., labeling, observation, analogies, classification, webbing, comparison, circle logic, syllogisms, cause and effect, patterning, sequencing, table logic, matrix logic). Students enjoy logic puzzles so much that they request more of them!

But how can a teacher justify using logic puzzles when standards must be met? Do you have students who finish assignments quickly (especially math assignments) and then ask, "What should I do now?" What if you had a logic book that reinforced math concepts?

This book is unique in that it requires students to use logical reasoning and perform a variety of operations and skills that align with state and national math standards (including standards for fractions, decimals, estimating, exponents, sequencing, algebra, time, percentages, measurement, area, and money). Students will read for details, make hypotheses, draw conclusions, organize information, and use syllogistic thinking. Teachers can feel confident that they are providing high-level thinking and rigor while reinforcing required skills in a format that students enjoy.

As I was creating this book, I enlisted the help of real students, who field tested puzzles and suggested topics that other kids would enjoy. As noted in the Table of Contents, the earlier puzzles in the book are easier, whereas the later puzzles are more challenging.

Students should be able to work independently on these problems. They should read the explanation of the logic process, apply the strategies described on p. 4, try the sample problem, begin with simpler puzzles, heed the instructions in introductory paragraphs, and note any hints for solving.

The solutions provided contain step-by-step explanations of my own reasoning; however, other solvers may use different paths of reasoning that also yield correct solutions. Teachers and parents may use the included solutions as an answer key, or they may allow students to self-check and clarify their reasoning.

This book may be used as alternative work during compacting, as enrichment, in centers, or just for fun. Students may work alone, with partners, in small groups, or in whatever arrangement best suits the needs of teachers and students. A student who fully understands the reasoning of a particular puzzle could demonstrate it to the rest of the class.

I hope that this book will be a helpful resource for teachers who strive to provide challenging, applicable, and practical math enrichment that is enjoyable for students who love to think!

How to Solve the Math Bafflers

Logic is a kind of critical thinking, an essential life skill. Using logic within a given content area is an effective way to integrate critical thinking, problem solving, and higher level processes into your everyday thought. Solving the puzzles in *Math Bafflers* promotes logic, reading for detail, analysis, making assumptions, and drawing valid conclusions in complex, real-life situations. Individuals who have strong critical thinking skills can make sense out of multiple pieces of information.

Read the following typical family scenario:

> Betty's Tuesday saxophone lesson is 60 minutes earlier than Nadine's Thursday tennis lesson, but Betty's Thursday swimming lesson is 30 minutes later than Nadine's Wednesday trumpet lesson. Also, Everett's Monday tuba lesson is earlier than Nadine's Thursday tennis lesson, and Everett's Friday racquetball lesson is 60 minutes earlier than Nadine's Wednesday music lesson.

Whew! That seems overwhelming. However, by organizing that scenario into individual clues and placing the information in a visual format, students can easily make sense of that confusing schedule. The logic used to solve the puzzles in *Math Bafflers* is similar to matrix logic, but the graphic is different.

Steps for Solving a Math Baffler

1. Read the introductory paragraph. It outlines the situation and contains necessary information.
2. Read each clue and use the information to make corresponding changes to the chart.
3. Each column represents a specific person or part of the situation in the problem. When a clue mentions a certain person or thing shown in a column, circle the appropriate item(s) listed in that column. For example, if a clue says that Ben is 11 years old, then under "Ben," you should circle "11 years." Items in the same section that are above, below, or next to the circled item must be crossed out, because they are no longer possibilities (e.g., Ben cannot also be 10 years old or 12 years old). It is very important that you always remember to do this!

4. Also use the clues to cross out items in a column that do not belong or are not possibilities. For example, if a clue tells you that Alicia is not 12 years old, then under "Alicia," cross out "12 years."

5. When there is only one item remaining in a certain column or row, then circle it. There will not be any more clues about it.

6. Once you have only one item circled in each row of each section, and only one in each column within a section, then you have solved the puzzle.

7. Check the solutions listed in the back of the book to make sure that you solved the puzzle correctly. If you have trouble solving a puzzle, or if you get incorrect answers, then read the description in the back of the book about how the puzzle could be solved. (It is possible, however, to solve the puzzle using slightly different reasoning.) At the end of each description in the Solutions section is a summary listing only the correct answers.

Strategies to Help You Solve the Math Bafflers

1. Always read introductory paragraphs. This paragraph describes the situation, and it may contain essential information that is not available in a clue. For example, the introductory paragraph might say, "Three students (a girl named Avery, a girl named Chris, and a boy named Pat) live in Napa." Then, a clue might tell you that a girl lives on Ash Street. After reading the introductory paragraph, you know that because Pat is a boy, he cannot live on Ash Street.

2. Be alert for clues about gender. Avery, Chris, and Pat are not gender-specific names. Recall introductory information when marking for a clue, such as "The girls do not like grapes." From the introduction, you know that Pat is a boy, so he likes grapes. Notice details such as gender pronouns in clues. For example, "*His* wallet contained $6.45." This means that a boy has $6.45, so no girl has $6.45.

3. Read, organize, and consider information from every clue. Each clue is essential for solving the puzzle. "Henry does not own a dog" may seem pointless. However, a later clue may tell you, "The one who owns the dog made $8 babysitting." Because Henry does not own a dog, he is not the one who made $8 babysitting.

4. There is sufficient information in the clues to solve every puzzle, but sometimes the logic is complex. Do not guess or assume. All of your conclusions should be backed up by proof from the clues and introductions.

5. Some of the Math Bafflers require you to perform mathematical calculations or fill in numbers. If you like, you should check the Solutions section in the back of the book to make sure you have the correct numbers before you go on to solve the puzzle.

6. Some puzzles can be solved from reading through all of the clues and doing the corresponding math operations just once. However, some of the Math Bafflers require you to go back and read through the clues again so that you can apply information from the later clues to the earlier clues. If necessary, reread clues and use further reasoning.

7. Use *syllogistic thinking* when you are marking items. *Syllogisms* have two premises and a conclusion. For example, one clue might say, "Susan drank half a cup of water." Another clue might say, "The one who drank half a cup of water ate ¼ of an apple." From these two premises, you can conclude that Susan ate ¼ of an apple.

8. Use *sequential thinking* to mark items with clues involving the order in which something happened. For instance, "Mary arrived after Jennifer, but before Connie." Write the different parts of the clue down in order: Jennifer, then Mary, and then Connie. A clue like "Roy is 2 years older than Fred, who is 3 years older than Susan" gives specific age differences. Write them in order. Then, once you know one age, you can get the others.

9. Notice items mentioned in multiple clues. Connect these pieces of information to draw conclusions.

10. A clue like "Neither Rob nor the nurse is 5 ft 9 in. tall" gives you information about three different people: Rob isn't the nurse, the nurse isn't 5 ft 9 in., and Rob isn't 5 ft 9 in.

11. In a clue like "There are four people: one who spent $3, the girl with blue eyes, the one who bought a soda, and Tania," you know that you are talking about four different people and that none of these pieces of information overlap with others. The person who spent $3 is different than the girl with blue eyes, who is different than the one who bought a soda, who is not Tania (and Tania did not spend $3, does not have blue eyes, and so forth).

Practice Problem

Try the following sample puzzle. For each clue, cross out items that do not belong or are not possibilities. In the provided solutions, when something is in brackets, it means that whatever the brackets enclose was learned in an earlier clue. For example, [3] means that something relevant was learned in Clue

3. If something is in parentheses—or is followed by "(only one)"—it means that this is the only choice remaining in a column or row, and you should circle it. For example, "Miss Fay matches up with Wednesday (only one)" means that Wednesday is the only item not crossed out in either the row or column for Miss Fay, and you should circle it.

Three siblings are all both musically and physically talented. Each sibling has a private music lesson and a private sports lesson on a different day and time each week. Read the clues to discover the time that each sibling has his or her music lesson and sports lesson.

	Betty	Everett	Nadine	Clue 1: Betty's Tuesday saxophone lesson is 60 min earlier than Nadine's Thursday tennis lesson.
Music	3:30 p.m. 4:00 p.m. ~~5:30 p.m.~~	3:30 p.m. 4:00 p.m. 5:30 p.m.	3:30 p.m. 4:00 p.m. 5:30 p.m.	
Sports	4:30 p.m. 5:00 p.m. 6:00 p.m.	4:30 p.m. 5:00 p.m. 6:00 p.m.	4:30 p.m. 5:00 p.m. ~~6:00 p.m.~~	Reasoning: If Betty's music lesson were at 5:30, then Nadine's sport would be at 6:30, and that is not a choice. Cross out 5:30 for Betty's music time. Cross out 6:00 for Nadine's sport time (no 5:00 music for Betty).

	Betty	Everett	Nadine	Clue 2: Betty's Thursday swimming lesson is 30 min later than Nadine's Wednesday trumpet lesson.
Music	3:30 p.m. 4:00 p.m. ~~5:30 p.m.~~	3:30 p.m. 4:00 p.m. 5:30 p.m.	~~3:30 p.m.~~ 4:00 p.m. 5:30 p.m.	
Sports	4:30 p.m. ~~5:00 p.m.~~ 6:00 p.m.	4:30 p.m. 5:00 p.m. 6:00 p.m.	4:30 p.m. 5:00 p.m. ~~6:00 p.m.~~	Reasoning: If Nadine's music lesson were at 3:30, then Betty's sport would be at 4:00, and that is not a choice. Cross out 3:30 for Nadine's music time. Cross out 5:00 for Betty's sport time (no 4:30 music time for Nadine).

	Betty	Everett	Nadine
Music	3:30 p.m. 4:00 p.m. ~~5:30 p.m.~~	3:30 p.m. 4:00 p.m. ~~5:30 p.m.~~	~~3:30 p.m.~~ ~~4:00 p.m.~~ (5:30 p.m.)
Sports	~~4:30 p.m.~~ ~~5:00 p.m.~~ (6:00 p.m.)	4:30 p.m. 5:00 p.m. ~~6:00 p.m.~~	4:30 p.m. 5:00 p.m. ~~6:00 p.m.~~

Clue 3: Everett's Monday tuba lesson is earlier than Nadine's Thursday tennis lesson.

Reasoning: Nadine has a 4:30 or 5:00 sport [2], so Everett's music lesson is earlier than 5:00. Cross out his 5:30 music time. (Nadine's music lesson is at 5:30 because it is the only one remaining in that row, so circle it). Cross out the 4:00 music time for Nadine. Betty's sport is at 6:00, because it is 30 min later than Nadine's music lesson [2]. Circle it. Cross out Betty's 4:30 sport time. Cross out Everett's 6:00 sport time.

	Betty	Everett	Nadine
Music	~~3:30 p.m.~~ (4:00 p.m.) ~~5:30 p.m.~~	(3:30 p.m.) ~~4:00 p.m.~~ ~~5:30 p.m.~~	~~3:30 p.m.~~ ~~4:00 p.m.~~ (5:30 p.m.)
Sports	~~4:30 p.m.~~ ~~5:00 p.m.~~ (6:00 p.m.)	(4:30 p.m.) ~~5:00 p.m.~~ ~~6:00 p.m.~~	~~4:30 p.m.~~ (5:00 p.m.) ~~6:00 p.m.~~

Clue 4: Everett's Friday racquetball lesson is 60 min earlier than Nadine's Wednesday music lesson.

Reasoning: Nadine's music lesson is at 5:30 [3], so Everett's sport is at 4:30. Circle it. Cross out his 5:00 sport time and Nadine's 4:30 sport time. Nadine has a 5:00 sport (only one)—circle it. Betty's music lesson is at 4:00, because it is 60 min earlier than Nadine's 5:00 sport [1]. Cross out Betty's 3:30 music time. (Everett has a 3:30 music lesson.) Cross out Everett's 4:00 music time.

Solution: Betty, 4:00 music lesson, 6:00 sport; Everett, 3:30 music lesson, 4:30 sport; Nadine, 5:30 music lesson, 5:00 sport.

Congratulations for practicing your reasoning skills, and have fun solving these Math Bafflers!

The Dog Days of Summer

Summer Fitzpatrick loves her dog, Sunshine. She especially likes spending extra time with Sunshine during summer vacation from school. Although Summer does not watch television every day, summer vacation is a great time for her to catch up on watching some of her favorite cartoon shows. Guess what appears in her favorite cartoons—yes, dogs! Read each clue to see if you can match each celebrity dog with the time of day that it appears in one of Summer's favorite cartoons.

Clues:

1. Snoopy appears earlier in the day than Pluto does.
2. Summer almost always eats breakfast sometime between 7:30 a.m. and 9:30 a.m.
3. Scooby-Doo is never on TV during Summer's breakfast.
4. Snoopy and Odie are never seen on a 10:00 a.m. cartoon show.
5. Odie is on a cartoon show earlier in the day than Snoopy's show.
6. Summer almost always eats dinner sometime between 5:00 p.m. and 7:00 p.m.
7. Sometimes Summer watches Scooby-Doo or Underdog while eating dinner.
8. Underdog can be seen later in the day than Scooby-Doo.

Odie	Pluto	Scooby-Doo	Snoopy	Underdog
8:00–9:00 a.m.	8:00–9:00 a.m.	8:00–9:00 a.m.	8:00–9:00 a.m.	8:00–9:00 a.m.
8:30–9:30 a.m.	8:30–9:30 a.m.	8:30–9:30 a.m.	8:30–9:30 a.m.	8:30–9:30 a.m.
10:00–10:30 a.m.	10:00–10:30 a.m.	10:00–10:30 a.m.	10:00–10:30 a.m.	10:00–10:30 a.m.
4:30–5:30 p.m.	4:30–5:30 p.m.	4:30–5:30 p.m.	4:30–5:30 p.m.	4:30–5:30 p.m.
5:30–6:00 p.m.	5:30–6:00 p.m.	5:30–6:00 p.m.	5:30–6:00 p.m.	5:30–6:00 p.m.

Halloween Haul

It was Halloween—time for trick or treating and the resulting sugar frenzy. To provide a safe area for trick or treating, the city of Hagatha held a party for kids at the community center. After stopping at various spooky displays, playing games at the booths, and gathering treats at each stop, three girls had quite a selection of sweet treats. No girl had the same amounts of caramels, chocolate chunks, or gumdrops. (Hint: That means that if someone had 15 caramels, then she did not have 15 chocolate chunks or 15 gumdrops, so remember to cross out those options.) Use the clues to deduce how many of each type of candy each girl took home.

Clues:

1. Jellie had twice as many chocolate chunks as caramels.
2. Lollie had twice as many gumdrops as chocolate chunks.
3. Candi had twice as many caramels as gumdrops.
4. Jellie had more gumdrops than Lollie.

Candi Barr	Jellie Beane	Lollie Popp
15 caramels 30 caramels 60 caramels	15 caramels 30 caramels 60 caramels	15 caramels 30 caramels 60 caramels
15 chocolate chunks 30 chocolate chunks 60 chocolate chunks	15 chocolate chunks 30 chocolate chunks 60 chocolate chunks	15 chocolate chunks 30 chocolate chunks 60 chocolate chunks
15 gumdrops 30 gumdrops 60 gumdrops	15 gumdrops 30 gumdrops 60 gumdrops	15 gumdrops 30 gumdrops 60 gumdrops

Show Me the Talent!

Mr. Hastings, the school band director, invited students to perform solos during a special Talent Week. Students were eager to show their capabilities, but hesitant to be the first to perform. Two girls (Betty and Meg) and three boys (Lee, Tim, and Scott) played on Thursday. Can you use the clues to figure out the order in which the students played their solos, and which instrument each one played?

Clues:

1. Tim played before Scott.
2. Neither Scott nor Tim played tuba or piano.
3. Meg did not play trumpet.
4. A boy played the piano.
5. Betty did not use her mouth to play her instrument.
6. Meg played immediately before the pianist and immediately after the flutist.
7. A girl performed last.
8. The first soloist did not play the flute.

Betty	Lee	Meg	Scott	Tim
first	first	first	first	first
second	second	second	second	second
third	third	third	third	third
fourth	fourth	fourth	fourth	fourth
fifth	fifth	fifth	fifth	fifth
flute	flute	flute	flute	flute
percussion	percussion	percussion	percussion	percussion
piano	piano	piano	piano	piano
trumpet	trumpet	trumpet	trumpet	trumpet
tuba	tuba	tuba	tuba	tuba

Name:.. Date:...

I Can "Ad" Fractions

Mrs. Crouse, the Media Center Specialist, is considering ordering several new magazines at school. She received five sample magazines, each of which had 60 pages. She asked three girls (Courtney, Morgan, and Shannon) and two boys (Ellis and Riley) each to evaluate a magazine and to note how many pages of advertisements and articles that magazine contained. Mrs. Crouse was seeking magazines with a higher number of articles, and not so many ads. Use the clues to determine how many pages of ads and articles each student found.

First, calculate the fractions for how much of the 60-page magazine each page count makes up. (For example, 30 pages is $\frac{1}{2}$.) Do this by dividing the number of ads and articles by 60, the number of pages. You will get a decimal as an answer. Convert the decimal to a fraction. Some of these are done for you. Write the correct fractions in the column beside the number of ads and articles. (Hint: This fraction will mean how much of the whole magazine is taken up by ads or articles. That means that if somebody does not have $\frac{2}{5}$ of a magazine's worth of ads, then that person also does not have a magazine that is $\frac{3}{5}$ articles, because the articles and ads should add up to $\frac{5}{5}$, or one whole magazine.) For example, 6 pages of ads from a 60-page magazine is $\frac{6}{60}$ or $\frac{1}{10}$.

Clues:

1. Ellis is not the one who found that $\frac{1}{4}$ of a magazine was ads.
2. One student discovered that her magazine had articles on $\frac{5}{6}$ of the pages.
3. Courtney is not the student who counted $\frac{1}{12}$ or $\frac{1}{6}$ of a magazine as ad pages.
4. Ellis counted fewer pages of ads than Shannon, who counted fewer than Morgan.
5. Riley is not the one who evaluated the magazine with $\frac{1}{4}$ ads.
6. Morgan counted more pages of articles than Riley.
7. Courtney did not count $\frac{1}{5}$ pages of ads.

I Can "Ad" Fractions, continued

	Courtney	Ellis	Morgan	Riley	Shannon	Fraction
Number of Ad Pages	5	5	5	5	5	$\frac{1}{12}$
	10	10	10	10	10	$\frac{1}{6}$
	12	12	12	12	12	_____
	15	15	15	15	15	_____
	20	20	20	20	20	_____
Number of Article Pages	40	40	40	40	40	_____
	45	45	45	45	45	_____
	48	48	48	48	48	_____
	50	50	50	50	50	$\frac{5}{6}$
	55	55	55	55	55	$\frac{11}{12}$

New Kids on the Block

Five neighbors have moved to Amarillo within the past 6 years. Each one is a different age, and each has lived in Amarillo a different length of time. Use the clues to determine each child's age and how long he or she has lived in Amarillo.

Clues:

1. Joshua is twice as old as Camryn.
2. Joshua has lived in Amarillo half as long as Petra.
3. Lydia is half as old as Ozzie, and Ozzie is half as old as Petra.
4. Ozzie has lived in Amarillo half as long as Lydia.
5. Petra has lived in Amarillo 3 years longer than Joshua, who has lived in Amarillo 1 year longer than Lydia.

	Camryn	Joshua	Lydia	Ozzie	Petra
Age in Years	4	4	4	4	4
	6	6	6	6	6
	8	8	8	8	8
	12	12	12	12	12
	16	16	16	16	16
Years in Amarillo	1	1	1	1	1
	2	2	2	2	2
	3	3	3	3	3
	4	4	4	4	4
	6	6	6	6	6

Breakfast Buddies

Four neighbor girls meet at one another's houses for breakfast on Thursday mornings before school. Last Thursday, they had cereal squares and fruit. Use the clues to determine how many cereal squares and how many pieces of fruit each person consumed for breakfast.

Clues:

1. Cass had ⅓ as many fruit pieces as she had cereal squares.
2. Dominique had three fewer fruit pieces than Suzette.
3. Suzette had ½ as many fruit pieces as she had cereal squares.
4. Elianna had three fewer fruit pieces than Cass.
5. Dominique had ⅓ as many fruit pieces as she had cereal squares.

	Cass	Dominique	Elianna	Suzette
Cereal	18 squares 24 squares 27 squares 30 squares	18 squares 24 squares 27 squares 30 squares	18 squares 24 squares 27 squares 30 squares	18 squares 24 squares 27 squares 30 squares
Fruit	3 banana slices 6 strawberries 9 raisins 12 blueberries	3 banana slices 6 strawberries 9 raisins 12 blueberries	3 banana slices 6 strawberries 9 raisins 12 blueberries	3 banana slices 6 strawberries 9 raisins 12 blueberries

Let's Party

Four friends all have birthdays in July (on the 1st, the 19th, the 23rd, and the 28th). This year they compared everything about their birthdays, including what gifts they received, what their families did on their special day, what they ate, cards they received, and who was there to celebrate with them. Use the clues to discover how many birthday cards each friend received and how many people attended his or her birthday celebration.

Clues:

1. Glenda received two fewer birthday cards than Adrian.
2. The one who had five people over for his or her birthday got 18 cards.
3. Brianna had two more guests at her party than Leonard.
4. The one who received 12 cards had seven guests over for the party.
5. Leonard received two fewer cards than Brianna.
6. The one with three guests at the party did not have 14 cards.
7. Glenda had two more guests at her party than Brianna had at hers.

	Adrian	Brianna	Glenda	Leonard
Birthday Cards	12 14 16 18	12 14 16 18	12 14 16 18	12 14 16 18
Guests at Celebration	three five seven nine	three five seven nine	three five seven nine	three five seven nine

Easter Eggscursion

Four friends went on an Easter egg hunt in the park. Each child was an "egg-spert" at finding a different number of various colored eggs in different locations. However, each child seemed to collect eggs that were mainly one color and mostly in one location. Use the clues to "eggstract" information and find out "eggsactly" which color most of each child's eggs were, how many eggs he or she found, and the location where he or she found the most eggs.

Clues:

1. The one who collected mostly blue eggs did not find them under the teeter-totter.
2. Anoki did not find 32 eggs.
3. Zeta found mostly yellow eggs, but not under bushes or in flowerbeds.
4. Marc found most of his eggs near the merry-go-round. He had more eggs than Zeta.
5. De'Sean found mainly pink eggs. He collected fewer eggs than Anoki.
6. Anoki did not find most of her eggs in the garden. She did not find 28 eggs.

	Anoki	De'Sean	Marc	Zeta
Main Color	blue green pink yellow	blue green pink yellow	blue green pink yellow	blue green pink yellow
Main Location	bushes garden play equipment rocks	bushes garden play equipment rocks	bushes garden play equipment rocks	bushes garden play equipment rocks
Number of Eggs Found	16 eggs 24 eggs 28 eggs 32 eggs	16 eggs 24 eggs 28 eggs 32 eggs	16 eggs 24 eggs 28 eggs 32 eggs	16 eggs 24 eggs 28 eggs 32 eggs

What's for Lunch?

Three classmates sat by one another at lunch today. Each girl had brought a sack lunch on this particular day. Each girl's lunch consisted of a sandwich, a fruit, a vegetable, a dessert, and a beverage. The girls were learning about calories in science class and decided to calculate how many calories (cal) their lunches contained. Use the clues to learn which classmate brought which item for lunch, and add the items' calories.

Whose lunch had the fewest calories? _____

Whose lunch had the most calories? _____

Clues:

1. Angie's fruit contained more calories than Cammie's.
2. The one who drank chocolate milk brought broccoli for lunch.
3. Rachel consumed more calories from her beverage than Angie.
4. Rachel's vegetable had fewer calories than Angie's.
5. Cammie's beverage and dessert combined were 2 calories fewer than her sandwich, which was not p.b. and j.
6. There was a difference of 200 calories between Angie's dessert and her sandwich.
7. Rachel's dessert contained 50 more calories than her fruit.

Name:.. Date:..

What's for Lunch?, continued

	Angie	Cammie	Rachel
Beverage	skim milk (87 cal) orange juice (122 cal) choc. milk (158 cal)	skim milk (87 cal) orange juice (122 cal) choc. milk (158 cal)	skim milk (87 cal) orange juice (122 cal) choc. milk (158 cal)
Dessert	cupcake (137 cal) cookie (138 cal) Twinkie (150 cal)	cupcake (137 cal) cookie (138 cal) Twinkie (150 cal)	cupcake (137 cal) cookie (138 cal) Twinkie (150 cal)
Fruit	blueberries (43 cal) apple (76 cal) banana (88 cal)	blueberries (43 cal) apple (76 cal) banana (88 cal)	blueberries (43 cal) apple (76 cal) banana (88 cal)
Sandwich	p.b. and j. (274 cal) chicken (310 cal) ham (337 cal)	p.b. and j. (274 cal) chicken (310 cal) ham (337 cal)	p.b. and j. (274 cal) chicken (310 cal) ham (337 cal)
Vegetable	celery (14 cal) carrot (21 cal) broccoli (30 cal)	celery (14 cal) carrot (21 cal) broccoli (30 cal)	celery (14 cal) carrot (21 cal) broccoli (30 cal)

Natasha Knows Her Numbers

Natasha is very good at math. She especially likes trying difficult problems. Here is an example of the type of problem Natasha likes: 13 x ? = 65. The answer is 5, because 13 x 5 = 65. Natasha's older sister played a dice game with Natasha. She used four different colored dice with the numbers 1–6 on them. Natasha solved Problem 1. Then she rolled the four dice to see if any of them would show the correct answer to her problem. Each color was a different number. One die showed the correct answer. After solving Problem 2, Natasha rolled again, and a different color die showed the correct answer for Problem 2. Solve Problems 1 and 2 before moving on to find out which colored die showed the correct answer for each problem.

Clues:

1. Both times Natasha rolled the orange die, she rolled an odd number.
2. The purple die did not show a correct answer either time Natasha rolled it.
3. The white die did not show the correct answer for 15 x ? = 60.
4. Natasha rolled an even number with the pink die both times.
5. For 15 x ? = 60, the purple die showed a number that was one less than the correct answer.
6. The correct answer for 12 x ? = 36 was not shown by the orange die.
7. Natasha did not roll a 4 using the pink die for Problem 1.

	Orange	Pink	Purple	White
Problem 1 **12 x ? = 36** ? = _____	1 2 3 4	1 2 3 4	1 2 3 4	1 2 3 4
Problem 2 **15 x ? = 60** ? = _____	3 4 5 6	3 4 5 6	3 4 5 6	3 4 5 6

It's a "Fun" Raiser

Students at Sunbelt Elementary recently participated in a school fundraiser by selling frozen cookie dough. Four students (two girls, Ila and Kacey, and two boys, Hilton and Jason) particularly enjoyed this fundraiser. They were in four different homerooms and four different grades, and they raised different amounts in cookie dough sales. See if the clues can help you identify the facts about each of these four "fun" raisers.

Clues:

1. Kacey brought in more money from customers than Ila.
2. Hilton is in second grade.
3. Ila's homeroom is not #11.
4. The second grader's homeroom is not #6 or #11.
5. Ila did not bring in $24 in orders.
6. The student in homeroom #6 is not in third grade and did not have $43 in orders.
7. Ila is in a lower grade than the girl in homeroom #4.
8. The third grader did not have $52 in sales.
9. Jason had a lower amount in orders than Hilton.
10. The student in homeroom #8 did not turn in $52 in orders.

	Hilton	Ila	Jason	Kacey
Homeroom	#4 #6 #8 #11	#4 #6 #8 #11	#4 #6 #8 #11	#4 #6 #8 #11
Grade	first second third fourth	first second third fourth	first second third fourth	first second third fourth
Sales Total	$24 $35 $43 $52	$24 $35 $43 $52	$24 $35 $43 $52	$24 $35 $43 $52

B. F. F.

Best friends forever! That's how these eight girls in Mrs. Nicely's class feel about each other. Even though each girl really does like the other seven, each one is the very best friend of just one other girl. In fact, each pair wears a different color necklace that says "Best Friends," and each pair also has a lucky number that both girls share. Can you determine which girls are best friends and what each pair's lucky number is?

Clues:

1. Nami and her best friend's lucky number is not 7.
2. Neither Nami nor Carolynn is best friends with Faizah.
3. Malina does not share the lucky number 11 with her best friend.
4. Alana shares the lucky number of 20 with her best friend, who is either Betsy or Malina.
5. Toni and her best friend have either 3 or 7 as their special number.
6. Carolynn and her best friend like everything to involve the number 11.

Alana	Carolynn	Nami	Sasha
Betsy Faizah Malina Toni	Betsy Faizah Malina Toni	Betsy Faizah Malina Toni	Betsy Faizah Malina Toni
lucky #3 lucky #7 lucky #11 lucky #20	lucky #3 lucky #7 lucky #11 lucky #20	lucky #3 lucky #7 lucky #11 lucky #20	lucky #3 lucky #7 lucky #11 lucky #20

Name: .... Date: ....

I'm on Cloud Nine

Nine classmates, including four girls named Ella, Kara, Myah, and Opal, quizzed one another on multiples of 9 whose product is greater than 100. Nobody had the same two factors. Calculate these problems and write the answers in the column on the left. Then read the clues and figure out who found which multiple of 9. (Hint: It will be helpful to put the possibilities in sequential order in Clues 8 and 9.)

Clues:

1. Axel and Chad did not find 117 or 153 as the product.
2. Gary, Kara, and Opal did not find 135 or 144 when they multiplied their factors.
3. Jake, Kara, and Zack did not calculate 162 or 180 as the product.
4. Axel, Ella, and Jake did not get 126 or 135 when they multiplied their factors.
5. None of the girls had 171 as an answer.
6. Chad, Ella, and Opal did not have even-numbered products.
7. Jake, Kara, and Zack did not have odd-numbered products.
8. Jake's product was 9 less than Ella's, and Ella's product was 9 less than Kara's.
9. Myah's product was 9 more than Axel's, and Axel's product was 9 more than Gary's.

Answers	Axel	Chad	Ella	Gary	Jake	Kara	Myah	Opal	Zack
_____	9 x 12	9 x 12	9 x 12	9 x 12	9 x 12	9 x 12	9 x 12	9 x 12	9 x 12
_____	9 x 13	9 x 13	9 x 13	9 x 13	9 x 13	9 x 13	9 x 13	9 x 13	9 x 13
_____	9 x 14	9 x 14	9 x 14	9 x 14	9 x 14	9 x 14	9 x 14	9 x 14	9 x 14
_____	9 x 15	9 x 15	9 x 15	9 x 15	9 x 15	9 x 15	9 x 15	9 x 15	9 x 15
_____	9 x 16	9 x 16	9 x 16	9 x 16	9 x 16	9 x 16	9 x 16	9 x 16	9 x 16
_____	9 x 17	9 x 17	9 x 17	9 x 17	9 x 17	9 x 17	9 x 17	9 x 17	9 x 17
_____	9 x 18	9 x 18	9 x 18	9 x 18	9 x 18	9 x 18	9 x 18	9 x 18	9 x 18
_____	9 x 19	9 x 19	9 x 19	9 x 19	9 x 19	9 x 19	9 x 19	9 x 19	9 x 19
_____	9 x 20	9 x 20	9 x 20	9 x 20	9 x 20	9 x 20	9 x 20	9 x 20	9 x 20

Who Will Bee the Winner?

Students from four different attendance centers in Lyntown participated in a local spelling bee. Four boys each qualified for the final round with high scores in the preliminary rounds. They succeeded in spelling words such as "cacophony," "floriferous," "innuendo," and "pecuniary." Can you discover the scores each boy achieved during the semifinal and final rounds, as well as learn the name of each boy's school?

Clues:

1. Clark scored 1 point higher in the semifinals than he did in the finals.
2. Farrell is not from Lyndale School.
3. Sawyer accumulated 99 points in the finals. In the semifinals, he earned more points than Dakarai, but fewer than the boy from Lyndon.
4. In the semifinals, Sawyer scored 3 fewer points than the boy from Lynford.
5. The boy from Lynwood scored 3 fewer points than Sawyer in the semifinals.
6. Farrell scored lower than Dakarai in the finals.

	Clark	Dakarai	Farrell	Sawyer
School	Lyndale Lyndon Lynford Lynwood	Lyndale Lyndon Lynford Lynwood	Lyndale Lyndon Lynford Lynwood	Lyndale Lyndon Lynford Lynwood
Semifinals Score	92 95 97 98	92 95 97 98	92 95 97 98	92 95 97 98
Finals Score	94 96 98 99	94 96 98 99	94 96 98 99	94 96 98 99

Name:.. Date:..

Test Out This Hat

Three kids (two girls named Fedora and Trilby and a boy named Stetson) were each named after a different type of hat. Their parents always told them that their unique names were chosen because a head is the most important part of the body, and a hat sits on top of a head to protect it. As things turned out, each of the kids is a bright and productive student, so their names are appropriate for them. Last week, each student took a test in three different subjects, and each one earned a different score. Use the clues to match each student with his or her score on each test.

Clues:

1. Trilby scored 2 points higher on her science test than Fedora.
2. Stetson had 1 more point than Trilby on the math test.
3. Stetson earned 1 more point on the spelling test than Trilby.
4. Fedora scored 2 points higher on the science test than Stetson.
5. The one who got 19 points on the spelling test got 48 points on the math test.

		Fedora	Stetson	Trilby
Math	Score	48 / 50	48 / 50	48 / 50
		49 / 50	49 / 50	49 / 50
		50 / 50	50 / 50	50 / 50
Science	Score	25 / 30	25 / 30	25 / 30
		27 / 30	27 / 30	27 / 30
		29 / 30	29 / 30	29 / 30
Spelling	Score	18 / 20	18 / 20	18 / 20
		19 / 20	19 / 20	19 / 20
		20 / 20	20 / 20	20 / 20

Tourney Trophy Time

The annual spring kickball tournament was held last week. Students from five attendance centers in Nutmeg, MA, competed in the tournament. Each class was vying for the coveted championship title. Charles Cameron, student reporter and scorekeeper, officially concluded that no sixth-grade class had earned the same place as it had in fifth grade. Can you determine the placement for each class of sixth graders compared to its placement in fifth grade?

Clues:

1. Miss Bailey's class ended two places lower in sixth grade than it did in fifth.
2. Edgar's and Samms's classes each ended three places higher in sixth grade than in fifth.
3. The class that placed second in fifth grade placed third in sixth grade.
4. As fifth graders, Miss Bailey's students placed lower than Ms. Sarahz's students.
5. Mr. Clark's and Mrs. Edgar's classes were the champions in either fifth or sixth grade.

	Bailey	**Clark**	**Edgar**	**Samms**	**Sarahz**
Fifth-Grade Rank	first second third fourth fifth	first second third fourth fifth	first second third fourth fifth	first second third fourth fifth	first second third fourth fifth
Sixth-Grade Rank	first second third fourth fifth	first second third fourth fifth	first second third fourth fifth	first second third fourth fifth	first second third fourth fifth

The Pumpkin Patches

Forty girls are members of their local 4-H Club, where they develop their leadership, do hands-on learning activities, and conduct research. This year, all 40 girls grew pumpkins for their annual garden show. Various types of pumpkins were grown, and each girl was very pleased to show off her harvest. Judges weighed and evaluated each pumpkin. Nine blue ribbons were awarded for the best pumpkins. Use the clues to discover the weights of the top nine pumpkins.

Clues:

1. Andi's pumpkin was 2 lb lighter than Grace's and 2 lb heavier than Destiny's.
2. Bianca's pumpkin weighed 3 lb less than Isabel's.
3. Charise's pumpkin tipped the scale at 2 lb more than Bianca's and 2 lb less than Evalyn's.
4. Hagen's pumpkin was heavier than Charise's.

Andi	Bianca	Charise	Destiny	Evalyn	Francy	Grace	Hagen	Isabel
1 lb	1 lb	1 lb	1 lb	1 lb	1 lb	1 lb	1 lb	1 lb
2 lb	2 lb	2 lb	2 lb	2 lb	2 lb	2 lb	2 lb	2 lb
3 lb	3 lb	3 lb	3 lb	3 lb	3 lb	3 lb	3 lb	3 lb
4 lb	4 lb	4 lb	4 lb	4 lb	4 lb	4 lb	4 lb	4 lb
5 lb	5 lb	5 lb	5 lb	5 lb	5 lb	5 lb	5 lb	5 lb
7 lb	7 lb	7 lb	7 lb	7 lb	7 lb	7 lb	7 lb	7 lb
9 lb	9 lb	9 lb	9 lb	9 lb	9 lb	9 lb	9 lb	9 lb
11 lb	11 lb	11 lb	11 lb	11 lb	11 lb	11 lb	11 lb	11 lb
12 lb	12 lb	12 lb	12 lb	12 lb	12 lb	12 lb	12 lb	12 lb

Let's Hang Out

Four friends decided to hang out at the skate park together for the afternoon. Each wore a cap and jacket with numbers on them. One boy's jacket and cap had the same number on them. Use the clues to determine which jacket and cap each boy wore.

Clues:

1. One boy wore a #3 jacket and a #69 cap.
2. The #27 jacket was a pullover.
3. Draymond's jacket had the same number as Anton's cap.
4. Kip's lucky number was on both his jacket and cap.
5. Anton's jacket had the same number as Wyatt's cap.
6. Kip wore either the #3 or the #12 cap.
7. Wyatt's jacket was the only one without snaps.

		Anton	Draymond	Kip	Wyatt
Cap		#3	#3	#3	#3
		#12	#12	#12	#12
		#27	#27	#27	#27
		#69	#69	#69	#69
Jacket		#3	#3	#3	#3
		#12	#12	#12	#12
		#27	#27	#27	#27
		#69	#69	#69	#69

Birthday in Buffalo

Charlene Brown invited five friends to her birthday party—three girls named Eden, Jessamyn, and Lynley, and two boys named Benjie and Scout. Use the clues to figure out the gift that each guest brought and the amount of money that he or she spent on the gift.

Clues:

1. Benjie spent $3.38 more than the girl who bought a book.
2. The paints cost $3.38 more than the gift Jessamyn bought.
3. Eden spent $3.38 less on the flip-flops she decorated with rhinestones than the guest who bought the magic cards.
4. Lynley spent $3.38 more on a CD than Benjie spent on his gift.

Benjie	Eden	Jessamyn	Lynley	Scout
book	book	book	book	book
CD	CD	CD	CD	CD
flip-flops	flip-flops	flip-flops	flip-flops	flip-flops
magic cards	magic cards	magic cards	magic cards	magic cards
paint set	paint set	paint set	paint set	paint set
$4.29	$4.29	$4.29	$4.29	$4.29
$7.67	$7.67	$7.67	$7.67	$7.67
$9.49	$9.49	$9.49	$9.49	$9.49
$12.87	$12.87	$12.87	$12.87	$12.87
$16.25	$16.25	$16.25	$16.25	$16.25

Five Clubs

Special clubs help students feel involved and gain expertise in their areas of interest. Next week, several different clubs from Olan Hills School will meet. Each student pays a different amount of dues for his or her specific club. Read the clues to determine each student's first name, the amount of dues he or she pays to belong to a club, and the particular club meeting that he or she will attend.

Clues:

1. Acting club dues are $8.
2. Bruce's cousin is in acting club.
3. There are three blondes: one who pays $12 dues, Eugene, and the one in math club.
4. Of four students, one is in math club, one is Bruce, one is in speech club, and one is Rick.
5. Leana and the one who pays $5 dues live in the same neighborhood as the one who pays $10 dues.
6. Eugene does not pay $5 dues for his club.
7. Deanne is in chess club. She does not pay $12 dues.

Bruce	Deanne	Eugene	Leana	Rick
$5 dues	$5 dues	$5 dues	$5 dues	$5 dues
$8 dues	$8 dues	$8 dues	$8 dues	$8 dues
$10 dues	$10 dues	$10 dues	$10 dues	$10 dues
$12 dues	$12 dues	$12 dues	$12 dues	$12 dues
$15 dues	$15 dues	$15 dues	$15 dues	$15 dues
acting club	acting club	acting club	acting club	acting club
chess club	chess club	chess club	chess club	chess club
computer club	computer club	computer club	computer club	computer club
math club	math club	math club	math club	math club
speech club	speech club	speech club	speech club	speech club

Swing Sewing

Three parents of swing choir participants volunteered to help with costuming for the choir's upcoming performance. Each parent bought a different amount of floral, striped, and polka dot fabrics to use for the costumes. Fabric is sold by the yard, so to solve this puzzle, remember that 1 yd = 36 in. Convert the fractions below to inches, and write them in the empty boxes in the puzzle. Cross out both the fractions and the inches as you eliminate choices. Use the clues to determine the amount of fabric and type of pattern that each parent purchased and sewed.

Clues:

1. Ms. Bucklin bought a third as much polka dot fabric as floral fabric.
2. Mrs. Tuttle purchased half as much polka dot fabric as Mr. Oatts did of the floral.
3. Mr. Oatts got ½ yd more of the striped than the floral.
4. Mr. Oatts bought half as much polka dot fabric as Ms. Bucklin got of the floral fabric.
5. Mrs. Tuttle purchased ½ yd less of the floral than the striped fabric.

	Ms. Bucklin		Mr. Oatts		Mrs. Tuttle	
Floral	¼ yd	_____ in.	¼ yd	_____ in.	¼ yd	_____ in.
	⅓ yd	_____ in.	⅓ yd	_____ in.	⅓ yd	_____ in.
	⅜ yd	_____ in.	⅜ yd.	_____ in.	⅜ yd.	_____ in.
Polka Dot	⅑ yd	_____ in.	⅑ yd	_____ in.	⅑ yd	_____ in.
	⅛ yd	_____ in.	⅛ yd	_____ in.	⅛ yd	_____ in.
	⅙ yd	_____ in.	⅙ yd	_____ in.	⅙ yd	_____ in.
Striped	⅔ yd	_____ in.	⅔ yd	_____ in.	⅔ yd	_____ in.
	¾ yd	_____ in.	¾ yd	_____ in.	¾ yd	_____ in.
	⅞ yd	_____ in.	⅞ yd	_____ in.	⅞ yd	_____ in.

Time for Lunch

The Meyer triplets arrived home from preschool. Their mother had prepared sandwiches and other items for them. They could have their food, but only after they had all counted the seeds in their oranges, the chocolate chips in their cookies, the raisins in their little boxes, the M&M's® in their packets, and the baby carrots in their bags. Each child had a different number of each item, and nobody had the same number of any items. (Hint: This means that if you circle "10" for one person, then you should cross out "10" in the other boxes for him or her.) Use the clues to discover how many of each item the triplets had.

Clues:

1. Layne had two fewer orange seeds than Payne.
2. Jayne had three more raisins than Layne.
3. Layne had three more carrots than Jayne.
4. Jayne had four fewer chocolate chips than Payne.
5. Layne did not have 15 M&M's®.
6. The one who had 14 chocolate chips had 10 carrots.

	Jayne	Layne	Payne
Seeds in Oranges	3 seeds 5 seeds 7 seeds	3 seeds 5 seeds 7 seeds	3 seeds 5 seeds 7 seeds
Chips in Cookies	10 chips 14 chips 18 chips	10 chips 14 chips 18 chips	10 chips 14 chips 18 chips
Raisins in Boxes	18 raisins 21 raisins 24 raisins	18 raisins 21 raisins 24 raisins	18 raisins 21 raisins 24 raisins
M&M's® in Packets	10 M&M's® 14 M&M's® 15 M&M's®	10 M&M's® 14 M&M's® 15 M&M's®	10 M&M's® 14 M&M's® 15 M&M's®
Carrots in Bags	7 carrots 10 carrots 13 carrots	7 carrots 10 carrots 13 carrots	7 carrots 10 carrots 13 carrots

Waterford's Water Days

Five students from Hadyn Henry Osborn (H$_2$O) School competed in the annual water-carrying contest during Waterford's Water Days celebration. The event requires participants to tote buckets of water from a starting line down a 50-ft path. On each consecutive return trip, an additional quart of water is added to the bucket until the student can no longer carry the load the entire 50 ft. Use the clues to determine the order in which the students competed and the weight each was able to carry. Remember that 4 qt = 1 gal.

Who won the contest? _____

Clues:

1. Ann carried more weight than Fran.
2. Ann competed before Fran and Dan.
3. Jan competed after Stan.
4. Jan carried more weight than Stan and Ann.
5. Jan carried 3 qt more than Dan.
6. Jan competed three places before Dan.
7. Dan carried 2 qt less than Ann.
8. Dan competed two places after Ann.
9. Fran carried 4 qt less than Ann.

	Ann	Dan	Fran	Jan	Stan	Quarts
Order	first second third fourth fifth	first second third fourth fifth	first second third fourth fifth	first second third fourth fifth	first second third fourth fifth	
Total Carried	1 ¾ gal 2 gal 2 ¼ gal 2 ¾ gal 3 gal	1 ¾ gal 2 gal 2 ¼ gal 2 ¾ gal 3 gal	1 ¾ gal 2 gal 2 ¼ gal 2 ¾ gal 3 gal	1 ¾ gal 2 gal 2 ¼ gal 2 ¾ gal 3 gal	1 ¾ gal 2 gal 2 ¼ gal 2 ¾ gal 3 gal	_____ qt _____ qt _____ qt _____ qt _____ qt

Lucky Sevven

The Sevven family enthusiastically supports school-sponsored events. This year the children collected various items and took them to school for recycling and cash rebates for books and materials. Read the clues and calculate the multiples of seven to discover which family member collected which amount of education box tops, plastic bottle caps, and soda can tabs.

Clues:

1. Robert had seven fewer box tops than Anna, and Lyn had seven fewer than Jack.
2. Lyn had seven fewer caps than Jack, and Anna had seven fewer than Robert.
3. Jack had seven fewer can tabs than Anna, and Lyn had seven fewer than Robert.
4. Anna had 21 fewer box tops than Lyn had caps.
5. Jack had 21 fewer caps than Lyn had can tabs.
6. Jack had half as many box tops as can tabs.

	Anna	Jack	Lyn	Robert
Box Tops	28 box tops 35 box tops 42 box tops 49 box tops	28 box tops 35 box tops 42 box tops 49 box tops	28 box tops 35 box tops 42 box tops 49 box tops	28 box tops 35 box tops 42 box tops 49 box tops
Bottle Caps	56 caps 63 caps 70 caps 77 caps	56 caps 63 caps 70 caps 77 caps	56 caps 63 caps 70 caps 77 caps	56 caps 63 caps 70 caps 77 caps
Can Tabs	84 tabs 91 tabs 98 tabs 105 tabs	84 tabs 91 tabs 98 tabs 105 tabs	84 tabs 91 tabs 98 tabs 105 tabs	84 tabs 91 tabs 98 tabs 105 tabs

The Fine Art of Scheduling

At school, students have art once per week for 45 minutes, physical education twice per week for 45 min each time, and vocal music twice per week for 30 min each time. No special class meets on the same day as another, so scheduling is very complex. Can you determine what time of day each teacher's special class is scheduled?

Clues:

1. The class with art at 10:00 has phys. ed. at 9:15. It is not Mrs. Bremer's or Ms. Mills's class.
2. Mr. Clay's class has phys. ed. and art at the same time on two different days.
3. Mrs. Bremer's class has phys. ed. at 10:45, but does not have music at 8:30 or 9:30, and does not have art at 10:45 or 1:00.
4. The class with 10:00 art, which is not Miss Linn's, does not have music at 9:00 or 10:30.
5. Mr. Clay's class has phys. ed. later than Mrs. Bremer's class, but Mr. Clay's class does not have music at 8:30 or 9:00.
6. The class that has 8:30 phys. ed. has music at 10:00 on a different day.
7. One class has phys. ed. at 10:00, music at 10:30, and art at 10:45, but it is not Miss Linn's.

	Bremer	Clay	Jasper	Linn	Mills
Art	10:00 10:45 11:30 1:00 1:45	10:00 10:45 11:30 1:00 1:45	10:00 10:45 11:30 1:00 1:45	10:00 10:45 11:30 1:00 1:45	10:00 10:45 11:30 1:00 1:45
Music	8:30 9:00 9:30 10:00 10:30	8:30 9:00 9:30 10:00 10:30	8:30 9:00 9:30 10:00 10:30	8:30 9:00 9:30 10:00 10:30	8:30 9:00 9:30 10:00 10:30
Phys. Ed.	8:30 9:15 10:00 10:45 11:30	8:30 9:15 10:00 10:45 11:30	8:30 9:15 10:00 10:45 11:30	8:30 9:15 10:00 10:45 11:30	8:30 9:15 10:00 10:45 11:30

5K for Kendra

Five students at Grayson School (two boys named Andy and Logan and three girls named Ava, Carly, and Rachel) organized a 5K-run/walk benefit for a fellow student, Kendra Tillson, whose family's medical bills skyrocketed when she became ill. Read the clues and match each student with the time he or she clocked for the run/walk and the amount of money each one raised.

Clues:

1. Rachel raised twice as much as Andy.
2. Andy ran slower than Rachel.
3. Rachel ran 1:45 faster than the girl who donated $78.
4. Ava ran 3:35 slower than the boy who donated $234.

Andy	Ava	Carly	Logan	Rachel
17:21	17:21	17:21	17:21	17:21
19:06	19:06	19:06	19:06	19:06
22:41	22:41	22:41	22:41	22:41
24:26	24:26	24:26	24:26	24:26
28:01	28:01	28:01	28:01	28:01
$78	$78	$78	$78	$78
$96	$96	$96	$96	$96
$156	$156	$156	$156	$156
$192	$192	$192	$192	$192
$234	$234	$234	$234	$234

Yummy, Yummy, Yummy, I Got Food in My Tummy

Three siblings walked to a local restaurant to have lunch together. Each ordered a different-sized beverage, a different fried item, and a different sandwich. Each of these items cost a different amount. Read the clues and discover how much each sibling paid for each item in his or her lunch.

Clues:

1. Jeremy did not buy fried sweet potato sticks.
2. Owen spent $0.30 more than Jeremy on a beverage.
3. One paid $1.99 for a beverage and $1.25 for french fries.
4. Laurie spent $0.60 less than Owen on a sandwich.
5. The one who purchased the $1.69 beverage bought fried sweet potato sticks.
6. One spent $2.49 on a sandwich and $1 on onion rings.

	Jeremy	Laurie	Owen
Beverage	$1.69 $1.99 $2.29	$1.69 $1.99 $2.29	$1.69 $1.99 $2.29
Fried Item	$1.00 $1.25 $1.50	$1.00 $1.25 $1.50	$1.00 $1.25 $1.50
Sandwich	$1.89 $2.49 $3.09	$1.89 $2.49 $3.09	$1.89 $2.49 $3.09

Pick and Peck a Pie

The city of Piper has a new bakery. To advertise the new business, the owner held a tasting event during the bakery's debut week. Freshly baked mini pies were cut into four small pieces each and offered to five patrons (three men named Balboa, Carlos, and Trent and two women named Etsu and Nylah), who volunteered to eat the pieces as other customers shopped. Each volunteer ate a different number of pieces of different-flavored pies on different days of the week. Read the clues and determine how many pieces each person consumed on which day. Add the pieces mentioned in the clues and write the number in the "Pieces" column beside its equivalent fraction of pie. For example, 5 pieces = 1 ¼ pies.

Clues:

1. The day before Trent volunteered, a woman ate two pieces each of lemon, chocolate, gooseberry, and blackberry and one piece of pecan. She ate her pieces 2 days after another person had three pieces each of raisin and cherry, two pieces each of raspberry, peach, and apple, and one piece of pecan.

2. One person ate three pumpkin pieces, two each of cherry and blueberry, and one each of pecan, peach, banana, and raisin; this was later in the week than the one who tasted two pieces each of apple, key lime, and raisin and one piece each of pumpkin, lemon, rhubarb, and pineapple.

3. Nylah nibbled pieces the day before Balboa and the day after the man who had three pieces each of strawberry and raspberry, two pieces each of chocolate, pumpkin, and peach, and one piece each of raisin, key lime, and apple.

4. Three sampled pie on consecutive days: Balboa, then the one who ate nine pieces, and then Trent.

Pick and Peck a Pie, continued

	Monday	Tuesday	Wednesday	Thursday	Friday	Pieces
Volunteer	Balboa Carlos Etsu Nylah Trent	Balboa Carlos Etsu Nylah Trent	Balboa Carlos Etsu Nylah Trent	Balboa Carlos Etsu Nylah Trent	Balboa Carlos Etsu Nylah Trent	
Equivalent	2 ¼ pies	2 ¼ pies	2 ¼ pies	2 ¼ pies	2 ¼ pies	_____ pieces
	2 ½ pies	2 ½ pies	2 ½ pies	2 ½ pies	2 ½ pies	_____ pieces
	2 ¾ pies	2 ¾ pies	2 ¾ pies	2 ¾ pies	2 ¾ pies	_____ pieces
	3 ¼ pies	3 ¼ pies	3 ¼ pies	3 ¼ pies	3 ¼ pies	_____ pieces
	3 ¾ pies	3 ¾ pies	3 ¾ pies	3 ¾ pies	3 ¾ pies	_____ pieces

It's Quite the Quad-Athlon

Four athletes did amazingly well in Quail Valley's first quad-athlon (a variation on a traditional triathlon) by finishing all four events in a total of exactly 230 minutes. No one clocked the same amount of time in any of his or her four events. (Hint: This means that if you circle "40 min" for a person's event, then you can cross out all other 40-min times for his or her other events.) Use the clues to determine the athletes' times in each event. Remember that 1 hr = 60 min.

Clues:

1. Xantha spent the same amount of time swimming as Yazmine spent biking.
2. Yazmine and Wylie swam for a total of 1 ½ hr.
3. Wylie ran the same length of time that Zeke walked.
4. Xantha and Yazmine biked for a total of 2 hr.
5. Zeke walked half as long as he ran.
6. Wylie swam the same length of time that Yazmine ran.

	Wylie	Xantha	Yazmine	Zeke
Biking	40 min 50 min 60 min 80 min	40 min 50 min 60 min 80 min	40 min 50 min 60 min 80 min	40 min 50 min 60 min 80 min
Running	40 min 50 min 60 min 80 min	40 min 50 min 60 min 80 min	40 min 50 min 60 min 80 min	40 min 50 min 60 min 80 min
Swimming	40 min 50 min 60 min 80 min	40 min 50 min 60 min 80 min	40 min 50 min 60 min 80 min	40 min 50 min 60 min 80 min
Walking	40 min 50 min 60 min 80 min	40 min 50 min 60 min 80 min	40 min 50 min 60 min 80 min	40 min 50 min 60 min 80 min

Let's Go to Quick Treats

Six friends stopped at Quick Treats after school for a soda. Normally, prices are directly proportionate to the number of ounces (the 8-oz drink would cost $0.49, and prices would rise until you reached the 40-oz drink, which would cost $0.99). However, the new cashier charged everyone an incorrect price. Use the clues to deduce what size beverage each person purchased and how much he or she was incorrectly charged.

Clues:

1. Ferrol was charged $0.10 less than Gregor and $0.10 more than Dominique.
2. Ferrol drank less than Dominique, who drank less than Gregor.
3. Indigo drank twice as much as Herschel, and she was charged at least $0.40 more.
4. Braylon drank half as much as Dominique, who drank less than Indigo.
5. Braylon was charged $0.30 more than Dominique.
6. Ferrol was charged $0.20 more than normal for the quantity of her beverage.

Braylon	Dominique	Ferrol	Gregor	Herschel	Indigo
8 oz	8 oz	8 oz	8 oz	8 oz	8 oz
12 oz	12 oz	12 oz	12 oz	12 oz	12 oz
16 oz	16 oz	16 oz	16 oz	16 oz	16 oz
24 oz	24 oz	24 oz	24 oz	24 oz	24 oz
32 oz	32 oz	32 oz	32 oz	32 oz	32 oz
40 oz	40 oz	40 oz	40 oz	40 oz	40 oz
$0.49	$0.49	$0.49	$0.49	$0.49	$0.49
$0.59	$0.59	$0.59	$0.59	$0.59	$0.59
$0.69	$0.69	$0.69	$0.69	$0.69	$0.69
$0.79	$0.79	$0.79	$0.79	$0.79	$0.79
$0.89	$0.89	$0.89	$0.89	$0.89	$0.89
$0.99	$0.99	$0.99	$0.99	$0.99	$0.99

Name:.. Date:..............................

It's Not Pay Day, It's Field Day!

Students at Kendall School participated in Track and Field Day, in which each student competed in three field events (long jump, shot put, and high jump) in addition to at least one running event. Use the clues to find out the distances each student recorded for each field event.

You will need to convert distances in feet and inches to total inches and write your calculations into the grid. Remember that 1 ft = 12 in. To convert 23 ft 4 in. into only inches, you find out how many inches 23 feet is (23 x 12 = 276) and add the remaining 4 inches to get 280 inches.

Clues:

1. Avery's long jump was 2 in. farther than four times Kayla's high jump.
2. Drew threw the shot 3 ft less than nine times his high jump.
3. Sarah's long jump was half the distance that Avery threw the shot.
4. The distance Matt threw the shot was twice the distance Drew long jumped.
5. Kayla had 181 in. for one event, which was half her distance in another event.
6. Matt jumped 6 in. higher than Avery.
7. Matt threw 3 in. farther than Avery.

It's Not Pay Day, It's Field Day!, continued

	Distance in Feet/Inches	Avery	Drew	Kayla	Matt	Sarah
Long Jump	13 ft 7 ½ in.	_____ in.	_____ in.	_____ in.	_____ in.	_____ in.
	13 ft 9 in.	_____ in.	_____ in.	_____ in.	_____ in.	_____ in.
	14 ft 5 in.	_____ in.	_____ in.	_____ in.	_____ in.	_____ in.
	14 ft 10 in.	_____ in.	_____ in.	_____ in.	_____ in.	_____ in.
	15 ft 1 in.	_____ in.	_____ in.	_____ in.	_____ in.	_____ in.
Shot Put	27 ft 3 in	_____ in.	_____ in.	_____ in.	_____ in.	_____ in.
	27 ft 6 in.	_____ in.	_____ in.	_____ in.	_____ in.	_____ in.
	29 ft 8 in.	_____ in.	_____ in.	_____ in.	_____ in.	_____ in.
	30 ft 2 in.	_____ in.	_____ in.	_____ in.	_____ in.	_____ in.
	32 ft 3 in.	_____ in.	_____ in.	_____ in.	_____ in.	_____ in.
High Jump	3 ft 8 in.	_____ in.	_____ in.	_____ in.	_____ in.	_____ in.
	3 ft 10 in.	_____ in.	_____ in.	_____ in.	_____ in.	_____ in.
	3 ft 11 in.	_____ in.	_____ in.	_____ in.	_____ in.	_____ in.
	4 ft 2 in.	_____ in.	_____ in.	_____ in.	_____ in.	_____ in.
	4 ft 4 in.	_____ in.	_____ in.	_____ in.	_____ in.	_____ in.

Holiday Vacation

Students always look forward to holiday vacation days off from school. This year, five students, including two boys (Kory and Lukas), told the class that their families were planning a trip to another state during holiday break. Each family planned to use a different way to travel, and each planned to leave on a different date. Can you determine each student's destination, departure date, and mode of transportation?

Clues:

1. Lukas and the girl whose family will go to Minnesota will travel by either bus or minivan.
2. Astaire's family will leave 2 days later than the family going to Minnesota, and Kory's family will leave 2 days later than the family headed to Louisiana.
3. The family going by train will leave 2 days later than the bus riders.
4. Neither Kory's nor Astaire's family is the one who will drive its car to Ohio.
5. The family going to Georgia plans to ride the train.
6. The family with the minivan, which is not Astaire's, is not going to visit Louisiana.
7. One family will board its plane 2 days before another leaves for Ohio.
8. Two kids are NBA fans. One girl will attend a home Trailblazers game, and Candace will watch her cousin play a home game for the Timberwolves.

Holiday Vacation, continued

	Astaire	Candace	Kory	Lukas	Mylah
Destination	Georgia Louisiana Minnesota Ohio Oregon	Georgia Louisiana Minnesota Ohio Oregon	Georgia Louisiana Minnesota Ohio Oregon	Georgia Louisiana Minnesota Ohio Oregon	Georgia Louisiana Minnesota Ohio Oregon
Transportation	bus car minivan plane train	bus car minivan plane train	bus car minivan plane train	bus car minivan plane train	bus car minivan plane train
Date	Dec. 23 Dec. 24 Dec. 25 Dec. 26 Dec. 27	Dec. 23 Dec. 24 Dec. 25 Dec. 26 Dec. 27	Dec. 23 Dec. 24 Dec. 25 Dec. 26 Dec. 27	Dec. 23 Dec. 24 Dec. 25 Dec. 26 Dec. 27	Dec. 23 Dec. 24 Dec. 25 Dec. 26 Dec. 27

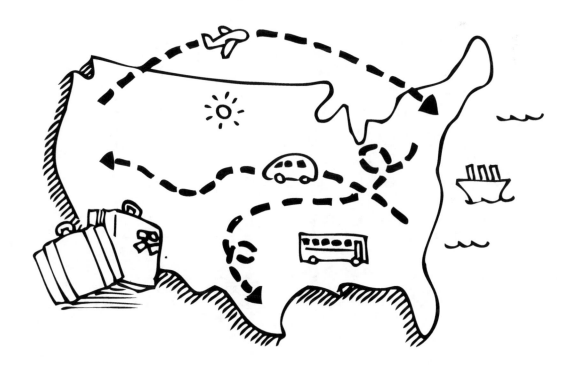

Name: ....   Date: ....

Cross Country Craze

Runners on the school's cross country team compete as individuals, with the seven fastest times from each team making up the team score. The middle school students run 3.2 kilometers (about 2 miles) on open grass, paths, mud, wooded areas, hills, and even through water. In high school, races are 5 km, about 3.1 mi. Four boys on the local team ran extremely well at yesterday's meet and placed in the top 15 finishers. Use the clues to find out the jersey number and shoe size of each boy, in addition to the place he achieved.

Clues:

1. Lloyd's jersey number is three less than Dale's jersey number.
2. The boy who wears size 10½ shoes earned 15th place.
3. Kyle finished eight places behind Dale.
4. The 11th-place finisher wears jersey #8.
5. Dale wears a half-size larger shoes than Kyle, but a smaller size than Tarkanian.
6. The third-place runner wears jersey #11.

		Dale	Kyle	Lloyd	Tarkanian
Jersey		#5	#5	#5	#5
		#8	#8	#8	#8
		#11	#11	#11	#11
		#14	#14	#14	#14
Shoe Size		10	10	10	10
		10 ½	10 ½	10 ½	10 ½
		11	11	11	11
		11 ½	11 ½	11 ½	11 ½
Place		3rd	3rd	3rd	3rd
		7th	7th	7th	7th
		11th	11th	11th	11th
		15th	15th	15th	15th

Greetings at the Meetings

Five friends recently organized a Youth Club. They have met every month from January–May, and a different boy or girl has hosted each meeting. The host planned refreshments and a social event, such as board games, card games, a sport, or dancing. At the first five meetings, the number in attendance ranged from 3–18 guests, in addition to the five organizers. Now that the word is spreading about the club, organizers anticipate that attendance will increase next month. Use the clues to find out which organizer hosted each meeting and how many kids attended each month.

Clues:

1. Adam did not host the night nine kids attended.
2. Grace hosted sometime before Jedd, but sometime after Cassandra.
3. Neither three nor 14 kids attended the meeting when Grace was hostess.
4. Adam was host 3 months after Kali. Neither meeting had three or seven kids attending.
5. Cassandra was hostess 2 months before the meeting that 18 kids attended, and Jedd hosted 1 month after the meeting with 18 kids.
6. Neither Cassandra nor Jedd hosted the meeting that nine kids attended.
7. Jedd hosted three people 1 month before Adam and 1 month after 18 people attended.

	Adam	Cassandra	Grace	Jedd	Kali
Attendance	3 guests 7 guests 9 guests 14 guests 18 guests	3 guests 7 guests 9 guests 14 guests 18 guests	3 guests 7 guests 9 guests 14 guests 18 guests	3 guests 7 guests 9 guests 14 guests 18 guests	3 guests 7 guests 9 guests 14 guests 18 guests
Month	January February March April May	January February March April May	January February March April May	January February March April May	January February March April May

Berry, Berry, Quite Culinary

Cinnamon Sage loves her unique name, and she has developed a love of cooking and baking that goes well with her culinary moniker. She especially enjoys adding fruits to cakes, coffee cakes, and muffins. None of her recipes call for the same quantities of any one fruit. (Hint: This means that if you deduce that one item uses 1 cup (1 c), then none of the other items will contain 1 c of that fruit, so you can cross them off.) Read the clues to determine how much fruit is needed for these three baked items.

Clues:

1. Cinnamon uses half as much fruit in her blueberry cake as she does in her apple cake.

2. Cinnamon puts half as much fruit in her apple coffee cake as she puts in her raisin coffee cake.

3. A smaller amount of fruit is put into Cinnamon's blueberry muffins than is put into her cranberry muffins, but it is more than is put into her apple muffins.

4. Cinnamon uses half as much fruit in her date cake as she does in her raisin cake.

5. Cinnamon puts half as much fruit in her date coffee cake as she does in her blueberry coffee cake.

6. Cinnamon uses ¼ c more fruit in her blueberry muffins than she does in her date coffee cake.

7. Cinnamon puts ¼ c more fruit in her blueberry cake than she does in her blueberry coffee cake.

8. A smaller amount of fruit is used in the apple muffins than is used in the raisin muffins.

Berry, Berry, Quite Culinary, continued

	Apple	Blueberry	Cranberry	Date	Raisin
Cake	1 c 1 ½ c 2 c 2 ½ c 3 c	1 c 1 ½ c 2 c 2 ½ c 3 c	1 c 1 ½ c 2 c 2 ½ c 3 c	1 c 1 ½ c 2 c 2 ½ c 3 c	1 c 1 ½ c 2 c 2 ½ c 3 c
Coffee Cake	½ c ⅝ c ¾ c 1 c 1 ¼ c	½ c ⅝ c ¾ c 1 c 1 ¼ c	½ c ⅝ c ¾ c 1 c 1 ¼ c	½ c ⅝ c ¾ c 1 c 1 ¼ c	½ c ⅝ c ¾ c 1 c 1 ¼ c
Muffins	½ c ⅔ c ¾ c ⅞ c 1 c	½ c ⅔ c ¾ c ⅞ c 1 c	½ c ⅔ c ¾ c ⅞ c 1 c	½ c ⅔ c ¾ c ⅞ c 1 c	½ c ⅔ c ¾ c ⅞ c 1 c

Name:.. Date:...

Kick, Pass, and Run

Four sisters entered the annual Kick, Pass, and Run Contest. Each trained hard for the following events: kicking a football, passing a football, and running as far as possible in 15 seconds while carrying a football. To apply each clue, convert yards to feet and inches (1 yd = 3 ft), working with fractions. For example, $\frac{1}{12}$ yd = 3 in., and $\frac{1}{6}$ yd = 6 in. Write the numbers in the boxes. Some are done for you. Read the clues to determine the distance each girl attained in each event of the contest.

Examples:

16 ¾ yd = 50 ft 3 in.
(16 yd x 3 = 48 ft, plus ¾ yd = 27 in. = 2 ft 3 in., which totals 48 ft + 2 ft + 3 in.)

21 ⅝ yd = 64 ft 8 in.
(21 yd x 3 = 63 ft, plus ⅝ yd = 20 in. = 1 ft 8 in., which totals 63 ft + 1 ft + 8 in.)

23 ⁵⁄₁₈ yd = 69 ft 10 in.
(23 yd x 3 = 69 ft, plus ⁵⁄₁₈ yd = 10 in., which totals 69 ft + 10 in.)

Clues:

1. Jade kicked 10 ft farther than Cheyenne passed.
2. Bekka kicked half as far as Sylvia ran.
3. Cheyenne ran 83 ft farther than Jade passed.
4. Bekka passed 22 ft shorter than Jade ran.
5. Sylvia kicked 20 ft farther than Cheyenne.

Math Bafflers: Grades 3–5 © Prufrock Press Inc. This page may be photocopied or reproduced with permission for student use.

Kick, Pass, and Run, continued

	Distance in Feet and Inches	Bekka	Cheyenne	Jade	Sylvia
Kicked	50 ft 3 in.	16 ¾ yd	16 ¾ yd	16 ¾ yd	16 ¾ yd
		19 ⅓ yd	19 ⅓ yd	19 ⅓ yd	19 ⅓ yd
		23 ⁵⁄₁₂ yd	23 ⁵⁄₁₂ yd	23 ⁵⁄₁₂ yd	23 ⁵⁄₁₂ yd
		27 ⁷⁄₁₂ yd	27 ⁷⁄₁₂ yd	27 ⁷⁄₁₂ yd	27 ⁷⁄₁₂ yd
Passed	64 ft 8 in.	21 ⁵⁄₉ yd	21 ⁵⁄₉ yd	21 ⁵⁄₉ yd	21 ⁵⁄₉ yd
		24 ¼ yd	24 ¼ yd	24 ¼ yd	24 ¼ yd
		32 ¹⁄₁₈ yd	32 ¹⁄₁₈ yd	32 ¹⁄₁₈ yd	32 ¹⁄₁₈ yd
		39 ½ yd	39 ½ yd	39 ½ yd	39 ½ yd
Ran	69 ft 10 in.	23 ⁵⁄₁₈ yd	23 ⁵⁄₁₈ yd	23 ⁵⁄₁₈ yd	23 ⁵⁄₁₈ yd
		38 ⅔ yd	38 ⅔ yd	38 ⅔ yd	38 ⅔ yd
		46 ⅚ yd	46 ⅚ yd	46 ⅚ yd	46 ⅚ yd
		49 ²⁄₉ yd	49 ²⁄₉ yd	49 ²⁄₉ yd	49 ²⁄₉ yd

Sisters Gone Shopping

Four sisters biked to the nearby mall and spent their paper route money on four items: a snack, a CD, a book, and some jewelry. Read the clues and match each sister with the amount she spent on each of the four items. Only one sister spent less than $50. You will need to add each girl's four items to know who it is.

Who spent less than $50? _____

Clues:

1. Danika spent $1 more than Nina on jewelry, but $1 less than Nina on snacks.
2. Nina spent $1 less than Kaiah on a CD, but $1 more than Kaiah on jewelry.
3. Danika spent $2 less than Nina on a book.
4. Kaiah spent $2 less than Nina on a snack.
5. The girl who spent $31.50 on jewelry bought a $13 CD.
6. The girl who spent $3.95 on a book bought a $14 CD.
7. Kaiah spent $1 less than Danika on a book.
8. Danika spent $2 more than Raythia on a snack.

Sisters Gone Shopping, continued

	Danika	Kaiah	Nina	Raythia
Total	$	$	$	$
Book	$2.95 $3.95 $4.95 $5.95	$2.95 $3.95 $4.95 $5.95	$2.95 $3.95 $4.95 $5.95	$2.95 $3.95 $4.95 $5.95
CD	$13 $14 $15 $16	$13 $14 $15 $16	$13 $14 $15 $16	$13 $14 $15 $16
Jewelry	$31.50 $32.50 $33.50 $34.50	$31.50 $32.50 $33.50 $34.50	$31.50 $32.50 $33.50 $34.50	$31.50 $32.50 $33.50 $34.50
Snack	$0.49 $1.49 $2.49 $3.49	$0.49 $1.49 $2.49 $3.49	$0.49 $1.49 $2.49 $3.49	$0.49 $1.49 $2.49 $3.49

Fetch, Fido

Four people (two girls named Kathy and Nancy and two boys named Joe and Pete) own dogs that have mastered two tasks at Ruff's Training School. Each dog fetched a stick of a certain length and dug up a buried bone of a different length. To solve the puzzle, calculate the lengths in inches for the centimeters listed below. Remember that 1 in. = 2.54 cm, so to find the inches, divide by 2.54.

Example:
10.16 cm = 4 in.
(10.16 ÷ 2.54 = 4)

13.97 cm = 5 ½ in.
(13.97 ÷ 2.54 = 5.5)

Write the numbers in the "Inches" column. Then use the clues to determine the lengths of the sticks and bones that each owner's dog fetched and dug up.

Clues:

1. One dog dug up the 11-in. bone and ran after the 2-in. stick.
2. The stick that Nancy's dog retrieved was 5 in. longer than the one Kathy's dog fetched.
3. The 3-in. bone was dug up by the dog that retrieved the 7-in. stick.
4. Pete's dog is not the one that brought his master the 11-in. bone.
5. One boy's dog dug up the 15-in. bone and brought him the 12-in. stick.
6. Joe's dog did not dig up the 3-in. or the 7-in. bone.

Fetch, Fido, continued

	Inches	Joe	Kathy	Nancy	Pete
Stick	_____ in.	5.08 cm	5.08 cm	5.08 cm	5.08 cm
	_____ in.	17.78 cm	17.78 cm	17.78 cm	17.78 cm
	_____ in.	30.48 cm	30.48 cm	30.48 cm	30.48 cm
	_____ in.	43.18 cm	43.18 cm	43.18 cm	43.18 cm
Bone	_____ in.	7.62 cm	7.62 cm	7.62 cm	7.62 cm
	_____ in.	17.78 cm	17.78 cm	17.78 cm	17.78 cm
	_____ in.	27.94 cm	27.94 cm	27.94 cm	27.94 cm
	_____ in.	38.10 cm	38.10 cm	38.10 cm	38.10 cm

Use these solutions to check students' work, or allow students to self-check.

To help teach logical thought, solutions are described step by step in the same order their clues appear. Please note that these solutions demonstrate the author's reasoning. You can use a different path of thinking and still get correct solutions. If you do not need help solving a given puzzle, you can skip to the end of the entry, where you will find a list of answers.

The introductions, charts, and clues included with each puzzle contain sufficient information to solve it. However, the logic required to solve some puzzles can be challenging. You may need more information to use a clue, so read the clues several times. If you are baffled, use the descriptions for help. Do not guess. Find information to verify your thinking.

Brackets indicate that relevant information was taken from an earlier clue. For example, [3] means that information from Clue 3 is being used. The use of parentheses or the notation "(only one)" indicates that this option is the only one remaining in a column or row, and you should circle it.

The Dog Days of Summer   p. 9

Clue 1: Snoopy is not on from 5:30–6:00. Pluto is not on from 8:00–9:00.
Clue 2: Use information later.
Clue 3: Scooby-Doo is not on at breakfast [2], so he is not on from 8:00–9:00 or 8:30–9:30.
Clue 4: Snoopy is not on from 10:00–10:30. Odie is not on from 10:00–10:30.
Clue 5: Odie is not on from 5:30–6:00. Snoopy is not on from 8:00–9:00.
Clue 6: Use information later.
Clue 7: Underdog and Scooby-Doo are on during dinner [6], so they are on from either 4:30–5:30 or 5:30–6:00. Eliminate Odie, Pluto, and Snoopy from those two times. Snoopy is on from 8:30–9:30 (only one). Then Odie is on from 8:00–9:00, and Pluto is on from 10:00–10:30 (only ones).
Clue 9: Underdog is on from 5:30–6:00, and Scooby–Doo is on from 4:30–5:30.
Answers: Odie, 8:00–9:00; Pluto, 10:00–10:30; Scooby-Doo, 4:30–5:30; Snoopy, 8:30–9:30. Underdog, 5:30–6:00.

Halloween Haul   p. 10

Clue 1: Jellie did not have 15 chocolate chunks or 60 caramels.
Clue 2: Lollie did not have 15 gumdrops or 60 chocolate chunks.
Clue 3: Candi did not have 15 caramels or 60 gumdrops.

Clue 4: Jellie did not have the fewest gumdrops (she had more than Lollie), so she did not have 15. Lollie did not have the most gumdrops. Then Lollie had 30 gumdrops (only one), Candi had 15 (only one), and Jellie had 60 (only one).

Further Reasoning: No girl had the same amount of each candy [Intro], so Candi did not have 15 chocolate chunks, Jellie did not have 60 chocolate chunks, and Lollie did not have 30 caramels or 30 chocolate chunks. You can see that Candi had 60 chocolate chunks, Jellie had 30 chocolate chunks, and Lollie had 15 chocolate chunks (only ones). Candi could not have 60 caramels [Intro], so she had 30. Jellie had 15 caramels, and Lollie had 60 caramels (only ones).

Answers: Candi, 30 caramels, 60 chocolate chunks, 15 gumdrops; Jellie, 15 caramels, 30 chocolate chunks, 60 gumdrops; Lollie, 60 caramels, 15 chocolate chunks, 30 gumdrops.

Show Me the Talent! p. 11

Clue 1: Tim did not play fifth. Scott did not play first.

Clue 2: Scott did not play piano or tuba. Tim did not play piano or tuba.

Clue 3: Meg did not play trumpet.

Clue 4: Piano was not Betty's or Meg's instrument [Intro, girls]. It was not Tim's or Scott's [2], so Lee played piano (only one).

Clue 5: Betty did not play flute, trumpet, or tuba, because they require a mouthpiece. She did not play piano [4], so she played percussion (only one). Meg played tuba (only one).

Clue 6: Meg was not first or fifth. Piano was not the first or second instrument played, and flute was not fourth or fifth. Lee played piano, so he was not first or second.

Clue 7: There are only two girls. Meg was not fifth [6], so Betty was fifth. Tim played first (only one).

Clue 8: Tim was first [7], so he did not play flute. He played trumpet, and Scott played flute (only ones).

Further Reasoning: The order [6] was flute [7, Scott], then Meg, then piano [4, Lee], so Scott played second, Meg played third, and Lee played fourth.

Answers: Betty, fifth, percussion; Lee, fourth, piano; Meg, third, tuba; Scott, second, flute; Tim, first, trumpet.

I Can "Ad" Fractions p. 12

Calculations: For ad pages, 5 pages = $\frac{1}{12}$; 10 pages = $\frac{1}{6}$; 12 pages = $\frac{1}{5}$; 15 pages = $\frac{1}{4}$; and 20 pages = $\frac{1}{3}$. For article pages, 40 pages = $\frac{2}{3}$; 45 pages = $\frac{3}{4}$; 48 pages = $\frac{4}{5}$; 50 pages = $\frac{5}{6}$; and 55 pages = $\frac{11}{12}$.

Clue 1: Ellis did not count 15 pages (¼) of ads, so he did not count 45 pages (¾) of articles.

Clue 2: The clue says "her" magazine was ⅚ (50 pages) articles, so it is not Ellis or Riley [Intro, boys], and Riley and Ellis did not count ⅙ (10 pages) ads.

Clue 3: Courtney's magazine was not $\frac{1}{12}$ (5 pages) or ⅙ (10 pages) ads, so it also was not $\frac{11}{12}$ (55 pages) or ⅚ (50 pages) articles.

Clue 4: Ellis did not count 15 pages (¼) or 20 pages (⅓) of ads [1], so he did not count 45 pages [1] or 40 pages (⅔) of articles. Shannon did not count 5 pages ($\frac{1}{12}$) or 20 pages (⅓) of ads, so she also did not count 55 pages ($\frac{11}{12}$) or 5 pages ($\frac{1}{12}$) of articles. Morgan did not count 5 pages ($\frac{1}{12}$) or 10 pages (⅙) of ads, so also did not count 50 pages (⅚) or 55 pages ($\frac{11}{12}$) of articles.

Clue 5: Riley did not count ¼ (15 pages) ads, so he also did not count ¾ (45 pages) articles.

Clue 6: Morgan did not count 40 pages (⅔) of articles (has more than Riley), and she did not count 50 pages (⅚) or 55 pages ($\frac{11}{12}$) [4], so she counted 48 pages (⅘) or 45 pages (¾) of articles. Riley did not count 55 pages ($\frac{11}{12}$) of articles (has less than Morgan), did not count 50 pages (⅚) [2], did not count 45 pages (¾) [5], and could not have counted 48 pages (⅘) of articles (Morgan's highest), so he must have counted 40 pages (⅔; only one) of articles and 20 pages (⅓) of ads.

Further Reasoning: Then Ellis counted 5 pages of ads and 55 pages of articles (only one). Shannon counted 10 pages of ads and 50 pages of articles (only one).

Clue 7: Courtney did not count ⅕ (12 pages), so Morgan counted ⅕ (12 pages) ads, meaning ⅘ articles. Then Courtney counted ¼ (15 pages) ads (only one), so she also counted ¾ (45 pages) articles.

Answers: Courtney, 15 pages (¼) ads, 45 pages (¾) articles; Ellis, 5 pages ($\frac{1}{12}$) ads, 55 pages ($\frac{11}{12}$) articles; Morgan, 12 pages (⅕) ads, 48 pages (⅘) articles; Riley, 20 pages (⅓) ads, 40 pages (⅔) articles; Shannon, 10 pages (⅙) ads, 50 pages (⅚) articles.

New Kids on the Block   p. 14

Clue 1: Joshua is not 4 or 6 years old, and Camryn is not 12 or 16 years old.

Clue 2: Joshua has not been in town 4 or 6 years, and Petra has not been there 1 or 3 years.

Clue 3: Lydia is not 12 or 16 years old, and Ozzie is not 4 or 6 years old. Ozzie is not 12 or 16 years old, so he is 8 years old. Then Lydia is 4 years old, and Petra is 16 years old. Camryn is 6 years old, and Joshua is 12 years old (only ones).

Clue 4: Lydia has not been in town 1 or 3 years, and Ozzie has not been there 4 or 6 years.

Clue 5: If Lydia has been in town 1 year, then Joshua has been there 2 years and Petra has been there 5 years (not a choice). This means Lydia has been there 2 years, Joshua has been there 3 years (half of Petra) [2], and Petra has been there 6 years. Then Ozzie has been in town 1 year (half of Lydia) [5], and Camryn has been in town 4 years (only one).

Answers: Camryn, age 6, 4 years in town; Joshua, age 12, 3 years in town; Lydia, age 4, 2 years in town; Ozzie, age 8, 1 year in town; Petra, age 16, 6 years in town.

Breakfast Buddies   p. 15

Clue 1: Cass had either 18 cereal squares and 6 pieces of fruit or 27 cereal squares and 9 pieces of fruit. She did not have 24 or 30 cereal squares or 3 or 12 pieces of fruit.

Clue 2: Suzette did not have 3 pieces of fruit. Dominique did not have 12 pieces of fruit.

Clue 3: Suzette had either 24 cereal squares and 12 pieces of fruit or 18 cereal squares and 9 pieces of fruit. She did not have 27 or 30 cereal squares or 6 pieces of fruit.

Clue 4: Cass did not have 3 or 12 pieces of fruit [1], so Elianna did not have 12 or 9 pieces of fruit. Then Suzette had 12 blueberries (only one).

Clue 5: Dominique had either 18 cereal squares and 6 pieces of fruit or 27 cereal squares and 9 pieces of fruit. She did not have 24 or 30 cereal squares or 3 bananas. Then Elianna had 3 banana slices (only one).

Further Reasoning: Reviewing Clue 2, Suzette had 12 pieces of fruit [4], so Dominique had 9 raisins, and Cass had 6 strawberries (only ones). Reviewing Clue 3, Suzette had 12 pieces of fruit, so she had 24 cereal squares. Reviewing Clue 5, Dominique had 9 pieces of fruit, so she had 27 cereal squares. Then Elianna had 30 cereal squares and Cass had 18 cereal squares (only ones).

Answers: Cass, 18 cereal squares, 6 strawberries; Dominique; 27 cereal squares, 9 raisins; Elianna, 30 cereal squares, 3 banana slices; Suzette; 24 cereal squares, 12 blueberries.

Let's Party   p. 16

Clue 1: Adrian did not get 12 cards. Glenda did not get 18 cards.

Clue 2: Glenda did not get 18 cards, so she did not have five people at the celebration.

Clue 3: Brianna did not have three guests. Leonard did not have nine guests.

Clue 4: Adrian did not get 12 cards [1], so he did not have seven guests.

Clue 5: Brianna did not get 12 cards. Leonard did not get 18 cards. Then Brianna did not have seven guests [4], and Leonard did not have five guests [2].

Clue 6: Use information later.

Clue 7: Glenda did not have three guests. Brianna did not have nine guests. Brianna had five guests (only one). Then Leonard had three guests [3], Glenda had seven guests, and Adrian had nine guests (only one).

Further Reasoning: Reviewing Clue 2, Briana had five guests, so she got 18 cards. Reviewing Clue 4, Glenda had seven guests, so she got 12 cards. Then Adrian got 14 cards [1]. Leonard got 16 cards [5] (only one).

Answers: Adrian, 14 cards, nine guests; Brianna, 18 cards, five guests; Glenda, 12 cards, seven guests; Leonard, 16 cards, three guests.

Easter Eggscursion   p. 17

Clue 1: Use information later.

Clue 2: Anoki did not find 32 eggs.

Clue 3: Zeta found yellow eggs, not in the bushes or the garden.

Clue 4: Marc found eggs in the play equipment, so Zeta found them in the rocks (only one). Marc did not find 16 eggs, and Zeta did not find 32 eggs.

Clue 5: De'Sean found pink eggs. De'Sean did not find 32 eggs, Anoki did not find 16, and Marc found 32 (only one).

Clue 6: Anoki did not find eggs in the garden, so she found them in the bushes, and De'Sean found them in the garden (only one). Anoki found 24 eggs (only one). De'Sean found fewer than she did [5], so he found 16, and Zeta found 28 (only one).

Further Reasoning: Reviewing Clue 1, blue eggs were not found near the play equipment, where Marc found eggs, so Marc did not find blue eggs. He found green eggs, and Anoki found blue eggs (only ones).

Answers: Anoki, blue, bushes, 24; De'Sean, pink, garden, 16; Marc, green, play equipment, 32; Zeta, yellow, rocks, 28.

What's for Lunch?   p. 18

Clue 1: Angie did not have 43 cal. Cammie did not have 88 cal.

Clue 2: Use information later.

Clue 3: Rachel did not have 87 cal. Angie did not have 158 cal.

Clue 4: Rachel did not have 30 cal. Angie did not have 14 cal.

Clue 5: Cammie had chocolate milk (158 cal) and a Twinkie (150 cal), totaling 308 cal (2 cal less than 310, so she had a chicken sandwich). Then Rachel had orange juice (122 cal) and Angie had skim milk (87 cal; only ones).

Clue 6: The only possibilities for Angie are that she had a cupcake (137 cal) and a ham sandwich (337 cal). Then Rachel had a cookie (138 cal) and a peanut butter sandwich (274 cal; only ones).

Clue 7: Rachel's dessert was a cookie [6] for 138 cal, and 138 cal – 50 cal = 88 cal, so Rachel had a banana for fruit (88 cal). Then Angie had an apple (76 cal) and Cammie had blueberries (43 cal; only ones).

Further Reasoning: Reviewing Clue 2, Cammie had chocolate milk [5], so she also had broccoli. Then Angie had a carrot (21 cal) and Rachel had celery (14 cal; only ones).

Answers: Angie, 87 cal, 137 cal, 76 cal, 337 cal, 21 cal; Cammie, 158 cal, 150 cal, 43 cal, 310 cal, 30 cal; Rachel, 122 cal, 138 cal, 88 cal, 274 cal, 14 cal. Totals: Angie, 658 cal; Cammie, 691 cal; Rachel, 636 cal. Rachel had the fewest calories, and Cammie had the most.

Natasha Knows Her Numbers   p. 20

Calculations: Problem 1: 12 x 3 = 36; Problem 2: 15 x 4 = 60.

Clue 1: Orange did not show a 2 or 4 for Problem 1, and orange did not show a 4 or 6 for Problem 2.

Clue 2: Purple did not show 3 for Problem 1 or 4 for Problem 2.

Clue 3: White did not show 4 for Problem 2.

Clue 4: Pink did not show 1 or 3 for Problem 1, and pink did not show 3 or 5 for Problem 2. Then pink showed the correct number, 4, for Problem 2 (only one).

Clue 5: Purple showed 3 for Problem 2. Then orange showed 5 for Problem 2, and white showed 6 for Problem 2 (only ones).

Clue 6: Orange did not show 3 for Problem 1, so orange showed 1, and white showed 3 (only ones).

Clue 7: Pink did not show 4 in Problem 1. Then pink showed 2 (only one), and purple showed 4.

Answers: Orange, 1, 5; pink, 2, 4; purple, 4, 3; white, 3, 6. White showed the correct answer for Problem 1, and pink showed the correct answer for Problem 2.

It's a "Fun" Raiser   p. 21

Clue 1: Kacey did not raise $24. Ila did not raise $52.

Clue 2: Hilton is in second grade.

Clue 3: Ila is not in room #11.

Clue 4: Hilton is the second grader [2], so he is not in room #6 or room #11.

Clue 5: Ila did not raise $24, so Ila raised either $35 or $43. Because Kacey had more money in orders than Ila [1], she must have raised more than $35, which is Ila's lowest possible amount, so she did not raise $35.

Clue 6: Use information later.

Clue 7: Ila is not in fourth grade. There is only one other girl [Intro, Kacey], so Kacey is in room #4. Then Hilton is in room #8, Ila is in room #6, and Jason is in room #11 (only ones).

Clue 8: Use information later.

Clue 9: Jason did not raise $52. Hilton did not raise $24. Then Jason raised $24 (only one).

Clue 10: Hilton is in room #8 [7], so he did not raise $52. Then Kacey raised $52 (only one).

Further Reasoning: Reviewing Clue 6, Ila is in room #6 [7], so she is not in third grade. Then she is in first grade (only one). Ila did not raise $43. Then she raised $35, and Hilton raised $43 (only ones). Reviewing Clue 8, we do not know who the third grader is, but we do know who had $52, and that is Kacey [10], so Kacey is not in third grade. She is in fourth grade, and Jason is in third grade (only ones).

Answers: Hilton, room #8, second grade, $43; Ila, room #6, first grade, $35; Jason, room #11, third grade, $24; Kacey, room #4, fourth grade, $52.

B. F. F.   p. 22

Clue 1: Nami's lucky number is not 7.

Clue 2: Nami is not best friends with Faizah. Carolynn is not best friends with Faizah.

Clue 3: Use information later.

Clue 4: Alana's lucky number is 20. Alana is not best friends with Faizah or Toni. Then Faizah is best friends with Sasha (only one).

Clue 5: Use information later.

Clue 6: Carolynn's lucky number is 11. Then Nami's lucky number is 3, and Sasha's is 7 (only ones).

Further Reasoning: Reviewing Clue 3, Malina's lucky number is not 11, but Carolynn's is [6], so Malina is not best friends with Carolynn. Reviewing Clue 5, Toni's lucky number is 3 or 7. Toni is not best friends with Alana [4]. Toni cannot be best friends with Carolynn, because her lucky number is 11. Toni cannot be best friends with Sasha, who is already best friends with Faizah. So Toni's lucky number is 3, and she is best friends with Nami. Then Alana is best friends with Malina, and Carolynn is best friends with Betsy (only ones).

Answers: Alana, Malina, 20; Carolynn, Betsy, 11; Nami, Toni, 3; Sasha, Faizah, 7.

I'm On Cloud Nine

Calculations: 9 x 12 = 108; 9 x 13 = 117; 9 x 14 = 126; 9 x 15 = 135; 9 x 16 = 144; 9 x 17 = 153; 9 x 18 = 162; 9 x 19 = 171; 9 x 20 = 180.

Clue 1: Axel and Chad did not find 9 x 13 (117) or 9 x 17 (153).

Clue 2: Gary, Kara, and Opal did not find 9 x 15 (135) or 9 x 16 (144).

Clue 3: Jake, Kara, and Zack did not find 9 x 18 (162) or 9 x 20 (180).

Clue 4: Axel, Ella, and Jake did not find 9 x 14 (126) or 9 x 15 (135).

Clue 5: Ella, Kara, Myah, and Opal [Intro, girls] did not find 9 x 19 (171).

Clue 6: Chad, Ella, and Opal did not find 108 (9 x 12), 126 (9 x 14), 144 (9 x 16), 162 (9 x 18), or 180 (9 x 20).

Clue 7: Jake, Kara, and Zack did not find 117 (9 x 13), 135 (9 x 15), 153 (9 x 17), or 171 (9 x 19).

Clue 8: Of Kara, Ella, and Jake, Kara had the highest number. We have already eliminated all numbers 135 and over for Kara, so the only combination that works is that Kara found 126, Ella found 117, and Jake found 108.

Clue 9: Of Myah, Axel, and Gary, Gary has the lowest number. We have already eliminated 144 and under for Gary. The combination of 153, 162, and 171 does not work (Myah did not find 171). The only combination that works is 162 for Gary, 171 for Axel, and 180 for Myah. Then Chad found 9 x 15 (135), Opal found 9 x 17 (153), and Zack found 9 x 16 (144; only ones).

Answers: Axel, 9 x 19; Chad, 9 x 15; Ella, 9 x 13; Gary, 9 x 18; Jake, 9 x 12; Kara, 9 x 14; Myah, 9 x 20; Opal, 9 x 17; Zack, 9 x 16.

Who Will Bee the Winner?

Clue 1: The only possible scores for Clark are 97 in the semifinals and 96 in the finals or 95 in the semifinals and 94 in the finals.

Clue 2: Farrell does not attend Lyndale.

Clue 3: Sawyer's finals score was 99. Sawyer and Dakarai do not attend Lyndon, because they have fewer semifinals points than the one from Lyndon, who scored either a 98 or a 97 in the semifinals. Sawyer scored a 97 or a 95 in the semifinals. Dakarai got a 95 or a 92 in the semifinals. Then Farrell scored a 98 in the semifinals (only one). Dakarai scored a 92 in the semifinals (only one).

Clue 4: Sawyer does not attend Lynford. Sawyer did not score a 97 in the semifinals (no 100), so he scored a 95 in the semifinals, and Lynford's student had a 98 in the semifinals, which was Farrell's score, so Farrell is from Lynford.

Clue 5: Sawyer scored a 95 in the semifinals, so Lynwood's student scored a 92, Dakarai's score, so Dakarai is from Lynwood. Then Sawyer is from Lyndale, and Clark is from Lyndon (only ones).

Clue 6: Dakarai did not score a 94 in the finals. Farrell did not score a 98 in the finals.

Further Reasoning: Reviewing Clue 1, Clark scored 97 points in the semifinals (only one), so he scored 96 points in the finals. Then Dakarai got 98 points in the finals, and Farrell got 94 points in the finals (only ones).

Answers: Clark, Lyndon, 97 semifinals, 96 finals; Dakarai, Lynwood, 92 semifinals, 98 finals; Farrell, Lynford, 98 semifinals, 94 finals; Sawyer, Lyndale, 95 semifinals, 99 finals.

Test Out This Hat   p. 25

Clue 1: In science, Trilby did not score 25, and Fedora did not score 29.

Clue 2: In math, Stetson did not score 48, and Trilby did not score 50.

Clue 3: In spelling, Stetson did not score 18, and Trilby did not score 20.

Clue 4: In science, Fedora did not score 25, and Stetson did not score 29. Fedora did not score 29 [1], so she scored 27 (only one). In science, Stetson scored 25 and Trilby scored 29 (only one).

Clue 5: Stetson did not score 48 in math [2], so he did not score 19 in spelling. He scored 20 in spelling (only one).

Further Reasoning: Reviewing Clue 3, Stetson scored 20 in spelling, so Trilby scored 19 in spelling. Fedora scored 18 in spelling (only one). Reviewing Clue 5, Trilby scored 19 in spelling, so she scored 48 in math. Reviewing Clue 2, Trilby scored 48 in math, so Stetson scored 49 in math, meaning that Fedora scored 50.

Answers: Fedora, 50 math, 27 science, 18 spelling; Stetson, 49 math, 25 science, 20 spelling; Trilby, 48 math, 29 science, 19 spelling.

Tourney Trophy Time   p. 26

Clue 1: Bailey's possibilities are first place (fifth grade) and third place (sixth grade), second place (fifth grade) and fourth place (sixth grade), or third place (fifth grade) and fifth place (sixth grade). Eliminate fourth and fifth places for fifth grade. Eliminate first and second places for sixth grade.

Clue 2: Edgar's possibilities are first place (sixth grade) and fourth place (fifth grade) or second place (sixth grade) and fifth place (fifth grade). Samms's possibilities are identical. Eliminate third, fourth, and fifth places for Edgar's and Samms's sixth-grade ranks. Eliminate first, second, and third places for Edgar's and Samms's fifth-grade rank. Because either Edgar's or Samms's class took first or second place in sixth grade, no other class could have been first or second. Eliminate Clark and Sarahz for first and second places in sixth grade. Because either Edgar's or Samms's class was fourth or fifth place in fifth grade, no other class could have been fourth or fifth. Eliminate Clark and Sarahz for fourth and fifth places in fifth grade.

Clue 3: Use information later.

Clue 4: Using Clue 1 information for Bailey, Sarahz's class could have been first or second place in fifth grade, meaning that Bailey's class would have been second or third place in fifth grade.

Clue 5: Edgar's class did not get first place in fifth grade [2], so it must have gotten first place in sixth grade. Samms's class must have gotten second place in sixth grade (only one). Clark's class was first place in fifth grade, so Sarahz's class must have been second place in fifth grade (only one), and Bailey's class was third place in fifth grade (only one).

Further Reasoning: Reviewing Clue 1, because Bailey's class was third in fifth grade, it was fifth in sixth grade. Reviewing Clue 2, because Edgar's class was first place in sixth grade, it got fourth place in fifth grade. Because Samms's class was second place in sixth grade, it took fifth place in fifth grade. Reviewing Clue 3, because Sarahz's class got second place in fifth grade, it got third place in sixth grade. Clark's class got fourth in sixth grade (only one).

Answers: Bailey, third place in fifth grade, fifth place in sixth grade; Clark, first place in fifth grade, fourth place in sixth grade; Edgar, fourth place in fifth grade, first place in sixth grade; Samms, fifth place in fifth grade, second place in sixth grade; Sarahz, second place in fifth grade, third place in sixth grade.

The Pumpkin Patches   p. 27

Clue 1: Destiny's pumpkin could have weighed 1 lb, 3 lb, 5 lb, or 7 lb. Andi's pumpkin could have weighed 3 lb, 5 lb, 7 lb, or 9 lb. Grace's pumpkin could have weighed 5 lb, 7 lb, 9 lb, or 11 lb. Destiny could not have had a 2-lb pumpkin, because that would mean that Andi's weighed 4 lb and Grace's weighed 6 lb (not a choice). Destiny could not have had a 4-lb pumpkin, because Andi would have had a 6-lb one and Grace would have had an 8-lb one (not choices).

Clue 2: Bianca could have had a pumpkin weighing 1 lb, 2 lb, 4 lb, or 9 lb. Isabel could have had one weighing 4 lb, 5 lb, 7 lb, or 12 lb.

Clue 3: Just as in Clue 1, the possibilities are that Bianca's pumpkin weighed 1 lb, 3 lb, 5 lb, or 7 lb. Charise's pumpkin could have weighed 3 lb, 5 lb, 7 lb, or 9 lb. Evalyn's could have weighed 5 lb, 7 lb, 9 lb, or 11 lb. However, in Clue 2, the possible weights for Bianca's pumpkin were 1 lb, 2 lb, 4 lb, and 9 lb, so the only possibility for Bianca's pumpkin's weight is 1 lb. This means that

Charise's pumpkin weighed 3 lb and Evalyn's weighed 5 lb. Then Destiny's weighed 7 lb, Andi's weighed 9 lb, and Grace's weighed 11 lb (only ones). Isabel's weighed 4 lb [2, 3 lb heavier than Bianca's].

Clue 4: Eliminate 2 lb for Hagen's pumpkin. Her pumpkin must have been heavier than Charise's, which weighed 3 lb. Her pumpkin weighed 12 lb (only one).

Answers: Andi, 9 lb; Bianca, 1 lb; Charise, 3 lb; Destiny, 7 lb; Evalyn, 5 lb; Francy, 2 lb; Grace, 11 lb; Hagen, 12 lb; Isabel, 4 lb.

Let's Hang Out   p. 28

Clues 1–5: Use information later.

Clue 6: Kip is not the #27 or the #69 cap. His jacket was not #27 or #69, either [4].

Clue 7: Use information later.

Further Reasoning: Reviewing Clue 1, Kip does not have a #69 cap [6], so he does not have a #3 jacket, meaning that he has a #12 jacket (only one). This means that he has the #12 cap [4]. Reviewing Clue 2, jacket #27 is the one without snaps, which is Wyatt's [7]. Wyatt's jacket is not #3, so his cap is not #69 [1]. Reviewing Clue 3, Draymond's jacket is not #12 or #27, so Anton's cap is not #12 or #27. Reviewing Clue 5, Wyatt's cap is not #12 or #69, so Anton's jacket is not #12 or #69. Then Anton's jacket is #3, so Wyatt's cap is #3. This means that Draymond has the #69 jacket (only one). Anton has the #69 cap [1] (only one). Draymond has the #27 cap (only one).

Answers: Anton, #69 cap, #3 jacket; Draymond, #27 cap, #69 jacket; Kip, #12 cap, #12 jacket; Wyatt, #3 cap, #27 jacket.

Birthday in Buffalo   p. 29

Clue 1: The book was not from Benjie or Scout [Intro, boys]. Benjie did not spend $4.29 (spent more than someone) or $9.49, because that is not $3.38 more than any other gift's price. The book cost either $4.29, $9.49, or $12.87, because those prices are $3.38 less than other given prices. You cannot mark anything yet, however. Use information later.

Clue 2: Paints cannot have cost $4.29 (not more than another price) or $9.49 (not $3.38 more), but you cannot mark anything here yet. Jessamyn spent $4.29, $9.49, or $12.87 ($3.38 less than another given price), so she did not spend $7.67 or $16.25. Jessamyn did not buy paints.

Clue 3: Eden bought flip-flops. Eden spent $4.29, $9.49, or $12.87 (all $3.38 less than another given price), so she did not spend $7.67 or $16.25. Magic cards cost $7.67, $12.87, or $16.25 (all $3.38 more than another given price), but you cannot mark this yet. Use information later.

Clue 4: Lynley bought a CD. Then Jessamyn bought a book (only one). Lynley spent $7.67, $12.87, or $16.25 (all $3.38 more than another given price). Benjie spent $4.29, $9.49, or $12.87 (all $3.38 less than another given price), but $4.29 and $9.49 were eliminated [1], so he spent $12.87 (only one). Then Lynley spent $16.25. Scout spent $7.67 (only one).

Further Reasoning: Reviewing Clue 1, the book cost $9.49 ($3.38 less than Ben's cost of $12.87), and Jessamyn bought the book, so Jessamyn spent $9.49. Eden spent $4.29 on flip-flops (only one). Reviewing Clue 2, Jessamyn's book cost $9.49, so paints cost $12.87, which is what Benjie spent, so he got paints. Scout got magic cards (only one).

Answers: Benjie, paint set, $12.87; Eden, flip-flops, $4.29; Jessamyn, book, $9.49; Lynley, CD, $16.25; Scout, magic cards, $7.67.

Five Clubs   p. 30

Clue 1: Use information later.

Clue 2: Bruce is not in acting club (his cousin is), so Bruce does not pay $8 [1].

Clue 3: The fact that these people are blondes is insignificant except to show that they are three different people. Eugene does not spend $12, $12 is not the amount of dues charged by math club, and Eugene is not in math club.

Clue 4: Bruce is not in math club or speech club. Neither is Rick.

Clue 5: The fact that these three live in the same neighborhood is insignificant except to show that they are three different people. Leana does not pay $5 or $10.

Clue 6: Eugene does not pay $5.

Clue 7: Deanne is in chess club. She does not pay $12. Then Bruce is in computer club, Rick is in acting club, Eugene is in speech club, and Leana is in math club (only ones).

Further Reasoning: Reviewing Clue 1, Rick is in acting club [7], so he pays $8 dues. Reviewing Clue 3, three different people match up with $12, Eugene, and math [7, Leana], so Leana does not pay $12. She pays $15 (only one). Then Eugene pays $10, Deanne pays $5, and Bruce pays $12 (only ones).

Answers: Bruce, $12, computer; Deanne, $5, chess; Eugene, $10, speech; Leana, $15, math; Rick, $8, acting.

Calculations:

Floral		Polka Dot		Striped	
¼ yd	9 in.	⅑ yd	4 in.	⅔ yd	24 in.
⅓ yd	12 in.	⅛ yd	4 ½ in.	¾ yd	27 in.
⅜ yd	13 ½ in.	⅙ yd	6 in.	⅞ yd	31 ½ in.

Clue 1: Bucklin's possibilities are ⅜ yd (13 ½ in.) floral and ⅛ yd (4 ½ in.) polka dot, or ⅓ yd (12 in.) floral and ⅑ yd (4 in.) polka dot. She did not buy ¼ yd (9 in.) floral, because ¹⁄₁₂ yd (3 in.) polka dot is not a choice. She did not buy ⅙ yd (6 in.) polka dot, because ½ yd (18 in.) floral is not a choice.

Clue 2: The possible combinations are that Oatts bought ⅓ yd (12 in.) floral and Tuttle bought ⅙ yd (6 in.) polka dot, or that Oatts bought ¼ yd (9 in.) floral and Tuttle bought ⅛ yd (4 ½ in.) polka dot. Oatts did not buy ⅜ yd (13 ½ in.) floral, because ³⁄₁₆ yd (6 ¾ in.) polka dot is not a choice. Tuttle did not buy ⅑ yd (4 in.) polka dot, because ²⁄₉ yd (8 in.) floral is not a choice.

Clue 3: This clue is about ½ yd (18 in.). Oatts's possibilities are ¾ yd (27 in.) striped and ¼ yd (9 in.) floral, or ⅞ yd (31 ½ in.) for Oatts's striped and ⅜ yd (13 ½ in.) for Oatts's floral. But Oatts did not buy ⅜ yd (13 ½ in.) floral [2]. Oatts did not buy ⅔ yd (24 in.) striped, because ⅙ yd (6 in.) floral is not a choice. Oatts did not buy ⅓ yd (12 in.) floral, because ⅚ yd (30 in.) is not a choice. So Oatts bought ¾ yd (27 in.) striped and ¼ yd (9 in.) floral.

Clue 4: It is possible that Bucklin bought ⅓ yd (12 in.) floral and Oatts bought ⅙ yd (6 in.) polka dot, or that Bucklin bought ¼ yd (9 in.) floral and Oatts bought ⅛ yd (4 ½ in.) polka dot. But Bucklin did not buy ¼ yd (9 in.) floral [1], so Oatts did not buy ⅛ yd (4 ½ in.) polka dot. Bucklin did not buy ⅜ yd (13 ½ in.) floral, because ³⁄₁₆ yd (6 ¾ in.) polka dot is not a choice. Oatts did not buy ⅑ yd (4 in.) polka dot, because ²⁄₉ yd (8 in.) floral is not a choice. So Bucklin bought ⅓ yd (12 in.) floral, and Oatts bought ⅙ yd (6 in.) polka dot. Then Tuttle bought ⅜ yd (13 ½ in.) floral and ⅛ yd (4 ½ in.) polka dot (only ones). Bucklin bought ⅑ yd (4 in.) polka dot (only one).

Clue 5: This clue is about ½ yd (18 in.). Mrs. Tuttle bought ⅜ yd (13 ½ in.) floral [4], so she bought ½ yd (18 in.) more striped, which is ⅞ yd (31 ½ in.). Then Ms. Bucklin bought ⅔ yd (24 in.) striped (only one).

Answers: Ms. Bucklin, ⅓ yd (12 in.) floral, ⅑ yd (4 in.) polka dot, ⅔ yd (24 in.) striped; Mr. Oatts, ¼ yd (9 in.) floral, ⅙ yd (6 in.) polka dot, ¾ yd (27 in.) striped; Mrs. Tuttle, ⅜ yd (13 ½ in.) floral, ⅛ yd (4 ½ in.) polka dot, ⅞ yd (31 ½ in.) striped.

Clue 1: Layne had 3 or 5 seeds (not 7), and Payne had 5 or 7 seeds (not 3). Because one of them had 5 seeds, Jane did not have 5.

Clue 2: Jayne had 21 or 24 raisins (not 18), and Layne had 18 or 21 raisins (not 24). Because one of them had 21 raisins, Payne did not have 21.

Clue 3: Layne had 10 or 13 carrots (not 7), and Jayne had 7 or 10 carrots (not 13). Because one of them had 10 carrots, Payne did not have 10.

Clue 4: Jayne had 10 or 14 chips (not 18), and Payne had 14 or 18 chips (not 10). Because one of them had 14 chips, Layne did not have 14.

Clue 5: Layne did not have 15 M&M's.

Clue 6: Payne did not have 10 carrots [3], so he could not have had 14 chips. Then he had 18 chips (only one). Layne had 10 chips, and Jayne had 14 chips (only ones). Because Jayne had 14 chips, she also had 10 carrots. Then Layne had 13 carrots, and Payne had 7 carrots (only ones).

Further Reasoning: Payne did not have 7 orange seeds, because he had 7 carrots [Intro, no one had the same number of any item], so he had 5 seeds. Layne had 3 seeds, and Jayne had 7 seeds (only ones). Jayne cannot have had 14 M&M's, because she had 14 chips [6], and she cannot have had 10 M&M's, because she had 10 carrots [6], so she had 15 M&M's. Layne cannot have had 10 M&M's, because he had 10 chips [6]. Layne had 14 M&M's, and Payne had 10 M&M's (only ones). Finally, Payne did not have 18 raisins, because he had 18 chips. He had 24 raisins (only one). Then Jayne had 21 raisins, and Layne had 18 raisins (only ones).

Answers: Jayne, 7 seeds, 14 chips, 21 raisins, 15 M&M's, 10 carrots; Layne, 3 seeds, 10 chips, 18 raisins, 14 M&M's, 13 carrots; Payne, 5 seeds, 18 chips, 24 raisins, 10 M&M's, 7 carrots.

Waterford's Water Days   p. 33

Calculations: 1 ¾ gal = 7 qt, 2 gal = 8 qt, 2 ¼ gal = 9 qt, 2 ¾ gal = 11 qt, 3 gal = 12 qt

Clue 1: Ann did not carry 1 ¾ gal. Fran did not carry 3 gal.

Clue 2: Ann was not fourth or fifth, and neither Fran nor Dan was first.

Clue 3: Jan was not first. Stan was not fifth.

Clue 4: Jan did not carry 1 ¾ gal or 2 gal. Stan did not carry 3 gal. Ann did not carry 3 gal.

Clue 5: Jan carried either 2 ¾ gal or 3 gal (11 qt or 12 qt). Dan carried either 2 gal or 2 ¼ gal (8 qt or 9 qt). Jan carried 12 qt (3 gal; only one), so Dan carried 9 qt (2 ¼ gal).

Clue 6: Jan was not third, fourth, or fifth, and she was not first [3], so she must have been second, meaning that Dan was fifth.

Clue 7: Dan carried 2 ¼ gal (9 qt) [5], so Ann carried 2 ¾ gal (11 qt).

Clue 8: Dan was fifth [6], so Ann was third. Fran was fourth, and Stan was first (only ones).

Clue 9: Because Ann carried 2 ¾ gal (11 qt) [7], Fran carried 1 ¾ gal (7 qt). Then Stan carried 2 gal (8 qt).

Answers: Ann, third, 2 ¾ gal; Dan, fifth, 2 ¼ gal; Fran, fourth, 1 ¾ gal; Jan, second, 3 gal; Stan, first, 2 gal.

Lucky Sevven   p. 34

Clue 1: Anna did not have 28 tops, and Robert did not have 49 tops. Jack did not have 28 tops, and Lyn did not have 49 tops.

Clue 2: Jack did not have 56 caps, and Lyn did not have 77 caps. Robert did not have 56 caps, and Anna did not have 77 caps.

Clue 3: Anna did not have 84 tabs. Jack did not have 105 tabs. Robert did not have 84 tabs. Lyn did not have 105 tabs.

Clue 4: Use information later.

Clue 5: Use information later.

Clue 6: If Jack had 98 tabs, then he had 49 box tops. He did not have 91 tabs (no 45 ½ box tops). If he had 84 tabs, then he had 42 box tops. He did not have 35 box tops (no 70 tabs).

Further Reasoning: Reviewing Clue 1, Jack did not have 35 box tops [5], so Lyn did not have 28 tops. Robert had 28 (only one), so Anna had 35 (7 more than Robert). Lyn had 42, and Jack had 49 (only ones). As a result, Jack had 98 can tabs [6]. Reviewing Clue 3, Jack had 98 can tabs, so Anna had 105 tabs. Robert had 91 tabs, and Lyn had 84 tabs (only ones). Reviewing Clue 4, Anna had 35 box tops, so Lyn had 56 bottle caps. Reviewing Clue 5, Lyn had 84 can tabs, so Jack had 63 bottle caps. Then Anna had 70 caps, and Robert had 77 caps (only ones).

Answers: Anna, 35 tops, 70 caps, 105 tabs; Jack, 49 tops, 63 caps, 98 tabs; Lyn, 42 tops, 56 caps, 84 tabs; Robert, 28 tops, 77 caps, 91 tabs.

The Fine Art of Scheduling   p. 35

Clue 1: Bremer and Mills do not have 10:00 art.

Clue 2: Clay does not have 1:00 or 1:45 art (no 1:00 or 1:45 phys. ed.) or 8:30 or 9:15 phys. ed. (no 8:30 or 9:15 art). Use information later.

Clue 3: Bremer has 10:45 phys. ed. Bremer does not have 8:30 or 9:30 music or 10:45 or 1:00 art. Because Clay does not have 10:45 phys. ed., he does not have 10:45 art [2].

Clue 4: Linn does not have 10:00 art.

Clue 5: Clay's music is not 8:30 or 9:00. His phys. ed. is 11:30 [3, Bremer's is 10:45], so his art is at 11:30 [2]. Then Bremer's art is at 1:45, and Jasper's art is at 10:00 (only ones). Because Jasper has 10:00 art, he has 9:15 phys. ed. [1], but not 9:00 or 10:30 music [4].

Clue 6: Bremer, Clay, and Jasper do not have 8:30 phys. ed., so they do not have 10:00 music.

Clue 7: Linn does not have 10:00 phys. ed., so she has 8:30 phys. ed. and 10:00 music [6]. Then Mills has 10:00 phys. ed. (only one), so she has 10:30 music and 10:45 art. Then Linn has 1:00 art (only one), Jasper has 8:30 music, Bremer has 9:00 music, and Clay has 9:30 music (only ones).

Answers: Bremer, 1:45 art, 9:00 music, 10:45 phys. ed.; Clay, 11:30 art, 9:30 music, 11:30 phys. ed.; Jasper, 10:00 art, 8:30 music, 9:15 phys. ed.; Linn, 1:00 art, 10:00 music, 8:30 phys. ed.; Mills, 10:45 art, 10:30 music, 10:00 phys. ed.

5K for Kendra   p. 36

Clue 1: Rachel raised either $156 or $192. Andy raised either $78 or $96.

Clue 2: Rachel did not finish in 28:01 (slowest time). Andy did not finish in 17:21 (fastest time).

Clue 3: Rachel finished in either 17:21 or 22:41 (only ones that are 1:45 faster than another given time), and $78 matches up with either 19:06 or 24:26 (cannot mark yet). A girl matches up with $78, so eliminate Andy and Logan. Then Andy raised $96 (only one), and Rachel raised $192 [1]. Andy cannot have run in 19:06 if Rachel ran 17:21, because a girl ran 1:45 slower than she did, and he cannot be 19:06 if Rachel ran 22:41, because she ran faster than him [2]. Eliminate 19:06 for Andy.

Clue 4: Ava ran 22:41 or 28:01 (only ones that are 3:35 slower than another given time), and $234 matches up with 19:06 or 24:26 (cannot mark yet). A boy raised $234, so eliminate Ava and Carly [Intro, girls], meaning that it was Logan (only one). Then Logan ran 19:06 or 24:26 (3:35 faster than Ava). The only girl who could have run 1:45 slower than Rachel [3] is Carly, so Carly ran either 19:06 or 24:26. Then Rachel ran 17:21 (only one), and Carly ran 19:06 and raised $78 [3]. Then Logan ran 24:26, and Ava raised $156 (only ones). Because Logan ran 24:26, Ava ran 28:01 (3:35 slower). Andy ran 22:41 (only one).

Answers: Andy, 22:41, $96; Ava, 28:01, $156; Carly, 19:06, $78; Logan, 24:26, $234; Rachel, 17:21, $192.

Yummy, Yummy, Yummy, I Got Food in My Tummy   p. 37

Clue 1: Use information later.

Clue 2: The possibilities are that Owen paid $2.29 and Jeremy paid $1.99, or Owen paid $1.99 and Jeremy paid $1.69. One of them had to have spent $1.99, so Laurie did not spend $1.99.

Clue 3: Either Owen or Jeremy spent $1.99 on a beverage, so one of them also spent $1.25 on french fries. Laurie did not.

Clue 4: The possibilities are that Owen paid $3.09 and Laurie paid $2.49, or Owen paid $2.49 and Laurie paid $1.89. One of them had to have spent $2.49, so Jeremy did not spend $2.49.

Clue 5: Owen did not buy the $1.69 beverage [2], so he did not get sweet potato sticks, but you cannot mark the price yet. Use information later.

Clue 6: Jeremy did not buy the $2.49 sandwich [4], so he did not get onion rings, which cost $1.00.

Further Reasoning: Reviewing Clue 1, if french fries cost $1.25 [3] and onion rings cost $1.00 [6], then sweet potato sticks must cost $1.50. Jeremy did not buy them, so he did not spend $1.50 on a fried item. He spent $1.25 (only one). Reviewing Clue 3, because Jeremy spent $1.25 on french fries, he also spent $1.99 on a beverage. Then Owen spent $2.29 [2] (only one). Laurie spent $1.69 (only one). Reviewing Clue 5, because Laurie spent $1.69 on a beverage, she also got sweet potato sticks, which cost $1.50. Then Owen spent $1.00 on onion rings (only one). Reviewing Clue 6, because Owen spent $1.00 on onion rings, he also spent $2.49 on a sandwich. Laurie's sandwich cost $1.89 [4] (only one), and Jeremy's sandwich cost $3.09 (only one).

Answers: Jeremy, $1.99 beverage, $1.25 fried item (french fries), $3.09 sandwich; Laurie, $1.69 beverage, $1.50 fried item (sweet potato sticks), $1.89 sandwich; Owen, $2.29 beverage, $1.00 fried item (onion rings), $2.49 sandwich.

Pick and Peck a Pie   p. 38

Calculations: 9 pieces = 2 ¼ pies; 10 pieces = 2 ½ pies; 11 pieces = 2 ¾ pies; 13 pieces = 3 ¼ pies; 15 pieces = 3 ¾ pies.

Clue 1: 3 ¼ pies (Monday or Tuesday) were eaten 2 days before a woman had 2 ¼ pies (Wednesday or Thursday) and a day before Trent ate pie (Thursday or Friday).

Clue 2: On Friday, 2 ½ pies were not eaten. On Monday, 2 ¾ pies were not eaten.

Clue 3: A man had 3 ¾ pies (Monday, Tuesday, or Wednesday). Nylah ate on Tuesday, Wednesday, or Thursday. Balboa ate on Wednesday, Thursday, or Friday. Eliminating 3 ¾ for Thursday and Friday leaves 2 ¾ for Friday (only one).

Clue 4: Balboa ate on Monday, Tuesday, or Wednesday in this clue, but he didn't eat on Monday or Tuesday [3], so his only possible day is Wednesday. Then 2 ¼ pies were eaten on Thursday, and Trent ate on Friday. Because 2 ¼ pies were eaten by a woman [1], no man ate on Thursday. Eliminate Carlos for Thursday.

Further Reasoning: Reviewing Clue 1, 2 ¼ pies were eaten on Thursday, and Trent ate on Friday, so 3 ¼ pies were eaten on Tuesday. Reviewing Clue 3, Balboa ate on Wednesday [4], so Nylah ate on Tuesday, and 3 ¾ pies were eaten on Monday. Then 2 ½ pies were eaten on Wednesday (only one). Etsu ate on Thursday (only one), and Carlos ate on Monday (only one).

Answers: Monday, Carlos, 3 ¾ pies; Tuesday, Nylah, 3 ¼ pies; Wednesday, Balboa, 2 ½ pies; Thursday, Etsu, 2 ¼ pies; Friday, Trent, 2 ¾ pies.

It's Quite the Quad-athlon   p. 40

Clue 1: Use information later.

Clue 2: One and a half hours is 90 min (50 + 40). Yazmine took 50 or 40 min, and Wylie took 50 or 40 min for swimming. Eliminate Xantha and Zeke for 40 and 50 min. Eliminate Wylie and Yazmine for 80 and 60 min. Because Xantha swam for 80 or 60 min [1], Yazmine's biking must have taken 80 or 60 min.

Clue 3: Use information later.

Clue 4: Two hours is 120 min (80 + 40). Xantha took 80 or 40 min, and Yazmine took 80 or 40 min for biking, but Yazmine did not take 40 min for biking [1, 2], so she took 80 min. Then Xantha took 40 min for biking. None of Xantha's other events took 40 min, and none of Yazmine's other events took 80 min [Intro]. Because Yazmine biked for 80 min, Xantha swam for 80 min [1]. None of Xantha's other events took 80 min [Intro]. Then Zeke swam for 60 min (only one), and none of Zeke's other events took 60 min. That leaves 50 min (only one) for Zeke's biking and 60 min for Wylie's biking (only one). None of Zeke's other events took 50 min, and none of Wylie's other events took 60 min [Intro].

Clue 5: Zeke walked for 40 min and ran for 80 min (only combination where one is half the other). Then Wylie walked 80 min (only one). Because Zeke walked for 40 min, Wylie ran for 40 min [3]. None of Wylie's other events took 40 min [Intro], so he swam for 50 min (only one). Yazmine swam 40 min (only one).

Clue 6: Because Wylie swam for 50 min, Yazmine ran for 50 min. Then Xantha ran for 60 min (only one). None of Yazmine's other events took 50 min, and none of Xantha's other events took 60 min [Intro]. Then Yazmine walked for 60 min, and Xantha walked for 50 min (only ones).

Answers: Wylie, 60 min biking, 40 min running, 50 min swimming, 80 min walking; Xantha, 40 min biking, 60 min running, 80 min swimming, 50 min walking; Yazmine, 80 min biking, 50 min running, 40 min swimming, 60 min walking; Zeke, 50 min biking, 80 min running, 60 min swimming, 40 min walking.

Let's Go to Quick Treats   p. 41

Clue 1: Gregor did not spend $0.49 or $0.59, Ferrol did not spend $0.49 or $0.99, and Dominique did not spend $0.89 or $0.99.

Clue 2: Ferrol did not get 32 or 40 oz, Dominique did not get 8 or 40 oz, and Gregor did not get 8 or 12 oz.

Clue 3: Indigo got 16, 24, or 32 oz, and Herschel got 8, 12, or 16 oz. Indigo did not spend $0.49, $0.59, $0.69, or $0.79, and Herschel did not spend $0.69, $0.79, $0.89, or $0.99.

Clue 4: Braylon got 8, 12, or 16 oz, Dominique got 16, 24, or 32 oz, and Indigo got 24 or 32 oz. Then Gregor got 40 oz (only one). As a result, Dominique could not have gotten 32 oz, so Braylon did not get 16 oz. (half of hers). Then Indigo got 32 oz (only one), and Hershel got 16 oz [3]. Then Dominique got 24 oz (only one), so Braylon got 12 oz (half), and Ferrol got 8 oz (only one).

Clue 5: Braylon spent $0.79, $0.89, or $0.99, and Dominique spent $0.49, $0.59 or $0.69. Then Ferrol did not spend $0.89, and Gregor did not spend $0.99 [1, $0.10 and $0.20 more].

Clue 6: The normal prices are $0.49 for 8 oz, $0.59 for 12 oz, and so on [Intro], but Ferrol paid $0.20 more than normal, so she did not pay $0.49 or $0.59. She paid $0.69 for 8 oz ($0.20 more than $0.49). Then Gregor paid $0.79 [1, $0.10 more], and Dominique paid $0.59 [1, $0.10 less]. Then Herschel paid $0.49 (only one).

Further Reasoning: Reviewing Clue 5, Dominique paid $0.59, so Braylon paid $0.89. Then Indigo paid $0.99 (only one).

Answers: Braylon, 12 oz, $0.89; Dominique, 24 oz, $0.59; Ferrol, 8 oz, $0.69; Gregor, 40 oz, $0.79; Herschel, 16 oz, $0.49; Indigo, 32 oz, $0.99.

Long Jump	Shot Put	High Jump
163 ½ in.	327 in.	44 in.
165 in.	330 in.	46 in.
173 in.	356 in.	47 in.
178 in.	362 in.	50 in.
181 in.	387 in.	52 in.

Clue 1: The only combination that works is 3 ft 8 in. (44 in.) x 4 = 176 in. + 2 in. = 178 in. (14 ft 10 in.), so Avery got 14 ft 10 in. (178 in.) in the long jump, and Kayla got 3 ft 8 in. (44 in.) in the high jump.

Clue 2: The only combination that works is 3 ft 11 in. (47 in.) x 9 = 423 in. − 36 in. = 387 in. (32 ft 3 in.), so Drew got 32 ft 3 in. (387 in.) in the shot put and 3 ft 11 in. (47 in.) in the high jump.

Clue 3: Sarah's long jump could have been 13 ft 7½ in. (163 ½ in.), 13 ft 9 in. (165 in.), or 15 ft 1 in. (181 in.), so Avery's shot put could have been 27 ft 3 in. (327 in.), 27 ft 6 in. (330 in.), or 30 ft 2 in. (362 in.). Eliminate 14 ft 10 in. and 14 ft 5 in. for Sarah, and 29 ft 8 in. and 32 ft 3 in. for Avery.

Clue 4: Matt's shot put could have been 27 ft 3 in. (327 in.), 27 ft 6 in. (330 in.), or 30 ft 2 in. (362 in.), so Drew's jump could have been 13 ft 7 ½ in. (163 ½ in.), 13 ft 9 in. (165 in.), or 15 ft 1 in. (178 in.). Drew did not get 14 ft 10 in. [1, Avery], so Matt did not get 29 ft 8 in. Eliminate 14 ft 5 in. for Drew, because 28 ft 10 in. is not a choice.

Clue 5: 181 in. is 15 ft 1 in., so that was Kayla's long jump, and her other event must been 30 ft 2 in. for shot put. Matt got 14 ft 5 in. in the long jump (only one).

Clue 6: Avery did not get 3 ft 8 in. (44 in.) [1, Kayla], so Matt did not get 4 ft 2 in. (50 in.). Avery must have gotten 3 ft 10 in. (46 in.), and Matt got 4 ft 4 in. (52 in.).

Clue 7: The only throw that works for Avery is 27 ft 3 in. (327 in.). Then Matt's throw was 27 ft 6 in. (330 in.). That leaves 29 ft 8 in. (356 in.) for Sarah.

Further Reasoning: Reviewing Clue 3, because Avery's shot was 27 ft 3 in. (327 in.), Sarah's long jump must have been 13 ft 7 ½ in. (163 ½ in.). Then Drew's jump was 13 ft 9 in. (165 in.; only one).

Answers: Avery, 178 in. (14 ft 10 in.), 327 in. (27 ft 3 in.), 46 in. (3 ft 10 in.); Drew, 165 in. (13 ft 9 in.), 387 in. (32 ft 3 in.), 47 in. (3 ft 11 in.); Kayla, 181 in. (15 ft 1 in.), 362 in. (30 ft 2 in.), 44 in. (3 ft 8 in.); Matt, 173 in. (14 ft 5 in.), 330 in. (27 ft 6 in.), 52 in. (4 ft 4 in.); Sarah, 163 ½ in. (13 ft 7 ½ in.), 356 in. (29 ft 8 in.), 50 in. (4 ft 2 in.).

Clue 1: Lukas did not take a car, plane, or train. Minnesota does not match up with Kory, Lukas [Intro, boys], car, plane, or train. Use information later.

Clue 2: Astaire does not match up with Minnesota, Dec. 23, or Dec. 24. Minnesota does not match up with Dec. 26 or Dec. 27. Kory does not match up with Louisiana, Dec. 23, or Dec. 24. Louisiana does not match up with Dec. 26 or Dec. 27. Use information later.

Clue 3: Train does not go with Dec. 23 or Dec. 24. Bus does not go with Dec. 26 or Dec. 27. Use information later.

Clue 4: Kory is not taking a car or going to Ohio. Astaire is not taking a car or going to Ohio. Whoever is taking a car is going to Ohio. Use information later.

Clue 5: Georgia goes with train. Use information later. Georgia does not go with Dec. 23 or Dec. 24 [3].

Clue 6: Astaire is not taking a minivan. Louisiana does not go with minivan. Use information later.

Clue 7: Plane does not go with Dec. 26 or Dec. 27. Ohio does not go with Dec. 23 or Dec. 24. Use information later.

Clue 8: The Trailblazers are from Portland, OR, and this clue is about a girl, so eliminate Kory and Lukas. Then Kory is going to Georgia (only one). The Timberwolves' home is Minneapolis, MN, so Candace is going to Minnesota, and she is not taking a car, plane, or train [1]. Because Lukas and Candace are the only ones who could take a bus or a minivan, nobody else goes with bus or minivan.

Further Reasoning: Reviewing Clue 5, Kory is going to Georgia [8], so Kory is taking a train. Then Astaire is taking a plane, and Mylah is taking a car (only ones), so Mylah is going to Ohio [4]. Then Lukas is going to Louisiana and Astaire is going to Oregon (only ones). Reviewing Clue 6, minivan does not go with Louisiana, and Lukas is going to Louisiana, so Lukas is not taking a minivan, he is taking a bus. Then Candace is taking a minivan (only one). Reviewing Clue 7, Astaire is taking a plane to Oregon, so Astaire is not leaving Dec. 26 or Dec. 27. She is leaving Dec. 25 (only one). Mylah is going to Ohio, so Mylah is not leaving Dec. 23 or Dec. 24. Reviewing Clue 2, Lukas is going to Louisiana, so Lukas is not leaving Dec. 26 or Dec. 27. Astaire is leaving Dec. 25, so Minnesota [8, Candace] goes with Dec. 23. Lukas is leaving Dec. 24 (only one). Lukas is going to Louisiana [2, Dec. 24], so Kory is leaving Dec. 26, and Mylah is leaving Dec. 27 (only one).

Answers: Astaire, Oregon, plane, Dec. 25; Candace, Minnesota, minivan, Dec. 23; Kory, Georgia, train, Dec. 26; Lukas, Louisiana, bus, Dec. 24; Mylah, Ohio, car, Dec. 27.

Cross Country Craze   p. 46

Clue 1: Dale does not wear jersey #5. Lloyd does not wear jersey #14.

Clue 2: Size 10 ½ will go with 15th place, but you do not know yet who that person is. Use information later.

Clue 3: Dale was not 11th or 15th. Kyle was not third or seventh.

Clue 4: Jersey #8 will go with 11th place, but you do not know yet who that person is. Use information later. Dale did not get 11th place [3], so he does not wear jersey #8.

Clue 5: Tarkanian wears larger shoes than at least two people, so he does not wear 10 or 10 ½. Dale does not wear the smallest or largest shoes, so he does not wear 10 or 11 ½. Kyle wears smaller shoes than at least two people, so he does not wear 11 or 11 ½.

Clue 6: Third place will go with jersey #11, but you do not know yet who this is. Use information later. Kyle did not come in third, so he does not wear jersey #11.

Further Reasoning: Reviewing Clue 1, Dale does not wear jersey #8, so Lloyd does not wear jersey #5. Reviewing Clue 2, either Dale or Kyle must wear size 10 ½ shoes [5], so one of them got 15th place [2]. Dale did not get 15th [3], so Kyle got 15th place and wears size 10 ½ shoes. Then Dale wears size 11 shoes (only one). Tarkanian wears size 11 ½ shoes (only one), and Lloyd wears size 10 shoes (only one). Reviewing Clue 3, Kyle got 15th place, so Dale got seventh place. Reviewing Clue 4, Kyle did not get 11th place, so he does not wear jersey #8. Reviewing Clue 6, Dale did not get third place, so he does not wear jersey #11. He wears jersey #14 (only one), and Lloyd wears jersey #11 [1]. Kyle wears jersey #5 (only one), and Tarkanian wears jersey #8 (only one). Reviewing Clue 4, Tarkanian wears jersey #8, so he was the 11th-place finisher. Then Lloyd got third place [6] (only one).

Answers: Dale, jersey #14, size 11 shoe, seventh place; Kyle, jersey #5, size 10 ½ shoe, 15th place; Lloyd, jersey #11, size 10 shoe, third place; Tarkanian, jersey #8, size 11 ½ shoe, 11th place.

Greetings at the Meetings   p. 47

Clue 1: Adam's meeting did not have nine guests.

Clue 2: Cassandra did not host in April or May (two hosted after). Grace did not host in January or May (one hosted before and after). Jedd did not host in January or February (two hosted before).

Clue 3: Grace's meeting did not have three or 14 guests.

Clue 4: The possibilities are that Kali hosted in January and Adam hosted in April, or that Kali hosted in February and Adam hosted in May. Kali did not host in March, April, or May, and her meeting was not attended by three or seven. Adam did not host in January, February, or March, and his meeting was not attended by three or seven.

Clue 5: Cassandra did not host in April or May [2] or in March (she hosted before at least three other people). In January, February, and May, there were not 18 guests, because the meeting with 18 guests must have taken place in either March or April. Jedd did not host in January, February, or March, because he hosted after at least three other people. Cassandra did not host for 18 people (hosted 2 months before the party for 18). Jedd did not host 18 (hosted a month after the party for 18). Kali did not host 18 (hosted in January or February [4], the months that do not match up with 18).

Clue 6: Cassandra and Jedd did not host for nine guests.

Clue 7: Jedd hosted three people. Jedd hosted in April or May [5], but he must have hosted in April, because Adam's month was after his, so Adam hosted in May. In March, 18 people attended. Grace hosted in March (only one), so she had 18 guests.

Further Reasoning: Cassandra hosted 2 months before the party with 18 [5], so she hosted in January. Kali hosted in February (only one). Adam hosted 14 people, Cassandra hosted seven people, and Kali hosted nine people (only ones).

Answers: Adam, 14, May; Cassandra, seven, January; Grace, 18, March; Jedd, three, April; Kali, nine, February.

Berry, Berry, Quite Culinary   p. 48

Clue 1: Blueberry cake uses either 1 ½ c or 1 c fruit, and apple cake uses either 3 c or 2 c.

Clue 2: Apple coffee cake uses either ⅝ c or ½ c, and raisin coffee cake uses either 1 ¼ c or 1 c.

Clue 3: Cranberry muffins do not use ½ c or ⅔ c fruit, and blueberry muffins do not use ½ c or 1 c. Apple muffins do not use ⅞ c or 1 c.

Clue 4: Date cake uses either 1 ½ c or 1 c, and raisin cake uses either 3 c or 2 c. Then cranberry cake uses 2 ½ c (only one).

Clue 5: Date coffee cake uses either ⅝ c or ½ c, and blueberry coffee cake uses either 1 ¼ c or 1 c. Then cranberry coffee cake uses ¾ c (only one). Cranberry muffins cannot use ¾ c [Intro, no same amounts].

Clue 6: Blueberry muffins use ⅞ c or ¾ c [3, not 1 c], and they do not use ⅔ c, so date coffee cake uses ½ c or ⅝ c [5, not ¾ c].

Clue 7: Blueberry cake uses 1 c or 1 ½ c [1], so blueberry coffee cake uses ¾ c or 1 ¼ c, but ¾ c coffee cake is cranberry, so 1 ¼ c of blueberries are used in coffee cake and 1 ½ c of blueberries are used in cake. Then there is 1 c of dates used in the cake and 1 c of raisins used in the coffee cake (only ones). So there cannot be 1 c of dates or raisins in the muffins [Intro]. There is 1 c of cranberries in muffins (only one).

Clue 8: There is not ½ c of fruit in the raisin muffins (the apple muffins have less).

Further Reasoning: Reviewing Clue 1, because there is 1 ½ c of blueberries used in the cake, there are 3 c of apples in the cake. Then there are 2 c of raisins in the cake (only one). Reviewing Clue 2, because there is 1 c of raisins in the coffee cake, there is ½ c of apples in the coffee cake. Then there is ⅝ c of dates in the coffee cake (only one). There cannot be ½ c of apples in the muffins [Intro], so there is ½ c of dates in the muffins (only one). Reviewing Clue 6, because there is ⅝ c of dates in the coffee cake, there is ⅞ c of blueberries in the muffins. Reviewing Clue 8, the largest amount for raisins in muffins is ¾ c., so there must be ⅔ cup of apples (less than raisins).

Answers: Apple, 3 c cake, ½ c coffee cake, ⅔ c muffins; blueberry, 1 ½ c cake, 1 ¼ c coffee cake, ⅞ c muffins; cranberry, 2 ½ c cake, ¾ c coffee cake, 1 c muffins; date, 1 c cake, ⅝ c coffee cake, ½ c muffins; raisin, 2 c cake, 1 c coffee cake, ¾ c muffins.

Kick, Pass, and Run   p. 50

Calculations: For kicking distances, 50 ft 3 in.; 58 ft; 70 ft 3 in.; 82 ft 9 in. For passing distances, 64 ft 8 in.; 72 ft 9 in.; 96 ft 2 in.; 118 ft 6 in. For running distances, 69 ft 10 in.; 116 ft; 140 ft 6 in.; 147 ft 8 in.

Clue 1: The only distances with a difference of 10 ft are 72 ft 9 in. (Cheyenne passed 24 ¼ yd) and 82 ft 9 in. (Jade kicked 27 ⁷/₁₂ yd).

Clue 2: The possibilities are that Bekka kicked 58 ft or 70 ft 3 in. (19 ⅓ yd or 23 ⁵/₁₂ yd), and that Sylvia ran 116 ft or 140 ft 6 in. (38 ⅔ yd or 46 ⅚ yd).

Clue 3: Jade passed 64 ft 8 in. (21 ⁵/₉ yd), and Cheyenne ran 147 ft 8 in. (49 ²/₉ yd; only ones with a difference of 83 ft).

Clue 4: Bekka passed 118 ft 6 in. (39 ½ yd), and Jade ran 140 ft 6 in. (46 ⅚ yd; only ones with a difference of 22 ft). Then Sylvia passed 32 ¹/₁₈ yd (96 ft 2 in.) and ran 38 ⅔ yd (116 ft; only ones). Then Bekka ran 23 ⁵/₁₈ yd (69 ft 10 in.;

Solutions

only one). Because Sylvia ran 38 ⅔ yd (116 ft), Bekka kicked 19 ⅓ yd (58 ft) [2].

Clue 5: Cheyenne kicked 50 ft 3 in. (16 ¾ yd), and Sylvia kicked 70 ft 3 in. (23 ⁵⁄₁₂ yd).

Answers: Bekka, kicked 19 ⅓ yd, passed 39 ½ yd, ran 23 ⁵⁄₁₈ yd; Cheyenne, kicked 16 ¾ yd, passed 24 ¼ yd, ran 49 ²⁄₉ yd; Jade, kicked 27 ⁷⁄₁₂ yd, passed 21 ⁵⁄₉ yd, ran 46 ⁵⁄₆ yd; Sylvia, kicked 23 ⁵⁄₁₂ yd, passed 32 ¹⁄₁₈ yd, ran 38 ⅔ yd.

Sisters Gone Shopping   p. 52

Clue 1: Danika did not spend $31.50 on jewelry or $3.49 on snacks. Nina did not spend $34.50 on jewelry or $0.49 on snacks.

Clue 2: Kaiah did not spend $13 on a CD or $34.50 on jewelry. Nina did not spend $16 on a CD or $31.50 on jewelry. Nina did not spend $34.50 on jewelry [1], so Kaiah did not spend $33.50 ($1 less than Nina).

Clue 3: Nina did not spend $2.95 or $3.95 on a book. Danika did not spend $4.95 or $5.95 on a book.

Clue 4: Nina did not spend $0.49 [1] or $1.49 on a snack. Kaiah did not spend $2.49 or $3.49 on a snack.

Clue 5: Neither Danika [1] nor Nina [2] spent $31.50 on jewelry, so neither bought the $13 CD. Kaiah did not buy a $13 CD [2], so she did not spend $31.50 on jewelry. Raythia spent $13 on a CD (only one) and $31.50 on jewelry. Then Kaiah spent $32.50 on jewelry, Nina spent $33.50 on jewelry, and Danika spent $34.50 on jewelry (only ones).

Clue 6: Nina did not spend $3.95 on a book, so she did not buy a $14 CD. She got a $15 CD (only one). Raythia got a $13 CD [5, not a $14 CD], so she did not buy a $3.95 book.

Clue 7: Danika did not spend $2.95 on a book. She did not spend $5.95 or $4.95 on a book [3], so she bought the $3.95 book, and Kaiah bought the $2.95 book. Then Danika got the $14 CD [6] and Kaiah got the $16 CD (only one).

Clue 8: Danika did not spend $3.49 [1], $0.49, or $1.49 (no amounts $2 less), so she spent $2.49 on a snack. Then Raythia spent $0.49 on a snack. Then Kaiah spent $1.49 and Nina spent $3.49 on snacks (only ones).

Further Reasoning: Reviewing Clue 3, Danika bought the $3.95 book [7], so Nina bought the $5.95 book. Raythia got a $4.95 book (only one). To solve the question, add the girls' totals for books, CDs, jewelry, and snacks.

Answers: Danika, $3.95 book, $14 CD, $34.50 jewelry, $2.49 snack; Kaiah, $2.95 book, $16 CD, $32.50 jewelry, $1.49 snack; Nina, $5.95 book, $15 CD, $33.50 jewelry, $3.49 snack; Raythia, $4.95 book, $13 CD, $31.50 jewelry, $0.49

snack. Totals (highest to least amount spent): Nina, $57.94; Danika, $54.94; Kaiah, $52.94; Raythia, $49.94. Raythia spent less than $50.

Fetch, Fido p. 54

Stick	2 in.	5.08 cm
	7 in.	17.78 cm
	12 in.	30.48 cm
	17 in.	43.18 cm
Bone	3 in.	7.62 cm
	7 in.	17.78 cm
	11 in.	27.94 cm
	15 in.	38.10 cm

Clue 1: Use information later.

Clue 2: Nancy's stick is not the shortest (2 in. or 5.08 cm). Kathy's stick is not the longest (17 in. or 43.18 cm).

Clue 3: Use information later.

Clue 4: Pete did not bury the 11-in. (27.94 cm) bone. Pete did not throw the 2-in. (5.08-cm) stick [1].

Clue 5: Kathy and Nancy [Intro, girls] did not bury the 15-in. (38.10-cm) bone or throw the 12-in. (30.48-cm) stick. A boy had those. Kathy did not throw the 12-in. (30.48-cm) stick, so Nancy did not have the 17-in. stick [2]. Nancy did not have the 12-in. (30.48-cm) stick, so Kathy did not have the 7-in. stick [2]. Then Nancy had the 7-in. (17.78-cm) stick (only one), so Kathy had the 2-in. (5.08-cm) stick.

Clue 6: Joe did not bury the 3-in. (7.62-cm) or the 7-in. (17.78-cm) bone.

Further Reasoning: Reviewing Clue 1, the 2-in. (5.08-cm) stick was thrown by Kathy [5], so Kathy buried the 11-in. (27.94-cm) bone. Joe buried the 15-in. (38.10-cm) bone (only one). Reviewing Clue 3, the 7-in. (17.78-cm) stick was thrown by Nancy [5], so Nancy buried the 3-in. (7.62-cm) bone. Pete had the 7-in. (17.78-cm) bone (only one). Reviewing Clue 5, the 15-in. (38.10-cm) bone belonged to Joe, so Joe buried the 12-in. (30.48-cm) stick. Pete had the 17-in. (43.18-cm) stick (only one).

Answers: Joe, 30.48-cm stick, 38.10-cm bone; Kathy, 5.08-cm stick, 27.94-cm bone; Nancy, 17.78-cm stick, 7.62-cm bone; Pete, 43.18-cm stick, 17.78-cm bone.